FAMOUS
lorida!

Famous Recipes from Famous Places

COUNTRY COOKIN'

D1515835

Joyce LaFray

© 1990 by Joyce LaFray

ALL RIGHTS RESERVED
No part of this book may be reproduced or
transmitted in any form or by any means,
electronic or mechanical, including photocopying,
recording, or by any information storage and
retrieval system, without permission in writing
from the publisher.

Manufactured in the United States of America

ISBN: 0-942084-41-1

FAMOUS FLORIDA!® **Country Cookin'** *introduces you to the best recipes from Florida's down-home backwoods eateries. By preparing these easy dishes in your home, you will experience taste sensations beyond your most diverse culinary adventures.*

These recipes, from Florida's favorite eateries, are a statement of Florida's heritage and its traditions in food preparation. You'll savor these recipes that are truly Floridian, as well as discovering another dimension of our beautiful Sunshine State.

Recipes include Key Lime Pie, of course, but collard greens, swamp cabbage, conch fritters and fried squash will most probably become staples in your own cooking repertoire. You'll enjoy recipes that have been handed down from generation to generation such as Sweet Potato Souffle, Fried Squash, Turnip Greens With Roots, Conch Fritters, Banana Duff, Home Fries, Poppy Seed Dressing, Scalloped Bananas and savory Cornmeal Muffins.

I know you'll delight in this collection of the **best** *of Florida "downhome" restaurants. Let us know how you fare!*

Joyce LaFray

From The Kitchen

FAMOUS FLORIDA!® *Country Cookin' offers you an exciting taste experience. Although many of these recipes are not your ordinary fare, they're a true taste of our native cuisine, and not to be forgotten!*

In many instances, special or unusual ingredients may be difficult to find and so we have included easy substitutions. However, some of the ingredients — such as armadillo, rattlesnake, and cooter, for instance — are not available at your local market. your best bet is to experience these recipes at the restaurants themselves.

If you plan to hunt the native fare yourself, be sure to check with county government regarding the local regulations. The Sabal Palm (Hearts of Palm) for instance, is not a state protected species, but many counties regulate and protect the species. Alligator is available in many restaurants, but is not sold over-the-counter to the consumer.

The recipes included in this cookbook have been very carefully selected and tested. Many have been reduced from large quantities to family-sized servings. In any event, the recipes are easy-to-prepare and some of the best you'll ever find!

Enjoy your tour of Florida Country Cooking!

Contents

NORTHEAST

NORTHWEST

FAMOUS *florida!*

Our sincere thanks to all of the restaurant owners and managers featured in this book for sharing their favorite recipes with us, without whom this book would not have been possible.

Allen's Historical Cafe

— *Auburndale* —

HUSHPUPPIES
(Allow to Chill Overnight)

2 T. sugar
¼ c. onions (minced)
2 c. yellow corn meal
1 c. white corn meal
½ T. salt
½ T. black pepper
1 t. baking powder
1½ c. buttermilk
  fat for frying

1. Mix all ingredients, except buttermilk and fat in large bowl.
2. Add buttermilk just until mixture is of a consistency to be rolled into small balls.
3. Let stand in refrigerator overnight. Can be kept in refrigerator, covered for several days.
4. Roll into small balls and drop into fat heated to 250°F. Cook until brown.

Makes: 4-5 dozen
Preparation: Chill overnight/10 minutes
Cooking: 15 minutes

"Fry up a batch and serve them with your favorite dish!"

— NOTES —

ALLEN'S CATFISH

small channel catfish, cleaned and scaled
salt
pepper
Accent
meal mixture
cooking oil for frying (Wesson or peanut oil)

—MEAL MIXTURE —
1   lb. yellow corn meal
½ lb. white corn meal
1   t. salt
½ t. black pepper

— MEAL MIXTURE —
1.   Mix all meal mixture ingredients together. (They can be stored in airtight container in refrigerator for several weeks.)
     — FISH —
2.   Sprinkle salt, pepper, and Accent over fish. Coat in meal mixture.
3.   Drop in oil heated to 350°F. Cook until nice and brown. (About 10-12 minutes.)

Serves: 1-2 fish per person
Preparation: 10 minutes
Cooking: 15 minutes

"One of Florida's favorite foods...And will soon be one of yours also!"

— NOTES —

RATTLESNAKE
(Allow to Freeze Overnight)

1 **rattlesnake**
1 **egg (beaten)**
breading mix
oil or Crisco for frying

1. Take the rattlesnake and lay it on a cutting board.
2. Remove the head plus at least two inches into the body in order to remove all poisons. Then run a knife along the belly of the snake (the skin comes off quite easily).
3. Clean out the inside of the snake and cut it into about 3″ pieces. Freeze these overnight.
4. When ready to prepare, remove from freezer. Allow to thaw slightly. Dip in egg, and breading mix.
5. Deep fat fry for 20 minutes in fat heated to 300°F.
6. The meat is similar to chicken or frog legs but very boney. Eat by picking the meat off the bones.

NOTE: Unless you are an expert rattlesnake hunter, we advise you NOT to hunt your own. A trip to Allen's may be your best bet on this one.

Serves: 4 oz. lean meat per serving
Preparation: Freeze overnight/20 minutes
Cooking: 20 minutes

"No wonder Rattlesnake hunts are so popular!"

— NOTES —

ARMADILLO

1 armadillo
2 c. water
¼ c. vinegar
    salt
    pepper
    flour
1-2 eggs (beaten)
    cooking oil for frying

1. To clean armadillo, hull from shell and remove tough skin from underside.
2. Combine water and vinegar in large bowl. Place meat in liquids to marinate for a few minutes.
3. Cut meat into small pieces, about 2" across.
4. Salt and pepper meat. Dip into flour, then into beaten egg, and back into flour.
5. Deep fat fry in cooking oil heated to 300°F for 20-25 minutes or until tender when tested with fork.

Serves: 4 oz. meat per serving
Preparation: 15 minutes
Cooking: 25 minutes

"Armadillo meat is somewhat dark in color but has a good flavor, resembling that of turtle! Come on, try it."

— NOTES —

COOTER (SOFT SHELL TURTLE)

3-4 turtles* (2 lbs.)
salt and pepper
Accent
flour
1 egg (beaten)
½ c. milk
fat for frying (enough to cover the turtles)

1. Take the turtles, turn them upside down and peel out the meat (like you peel an orange).
2. Clean it and cut it into small pieces.
3. Sprinkle with salt, pepper, and Accent.
4. Dip in flour, then in mixture of egg and milk, then back in flour.
5. Deep fat fry in fat heated to 300°F until done or southern fry in gravy.

Serves: 6
Preparation: 25 minutes
Cooking: 15-20 minutes

*Cooter is tender, unlike the sea turtle found in many Florida lakes.

"Has a similar taste to chicken but a lot better!"

— NOTES —

The Lincoln Restaurant

— *Tampa* —

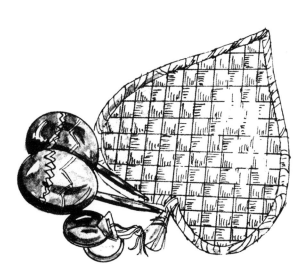

YELLOW RICE

¼	c. olive oil
1	Spanish onion (diced)
1	green pepper (diced)
1	clove garlic (crushed)
2	bay leaves
1	pinch oregano
2	t. salt
½	t. pepper
1	tomato (diced — may substitute 2 canned whole tomatoes crushed)
2	c. water (can include juice from canned tomatoes)
1	c. long grain rice (do not use converted)
2	drops yellow food coloring
	peas and pimiento (garnish)

1. Heat oil in large skillet. Add next 8 ingredients. Saute until tender.
2. Add water. Bring to boil. Add rice and food coloring.
3. Bring to boil again. Stir. Cover and bake in oven at 375°F for 20 minutes. Or cook on top of stove at medium-low for 20 minutes.
4. Garnish with peas and pimiento. Serve.

Serves: 4 as side dish; 2 as entree with meat
Preparation: 5 minutes
Cooking: 30 minutes

"Perfect with chicken!"

— NOTES —

CARNE CON PAPAS (SPANISH BEEF STEW)

1	lb. top round cubes
	olive oil for sauteing
2	t. salt
1	t. pepper
1	clove garlic (crushed)
1	28 oz. can whole tomatoes (crushed with hand)
1	large Spanish onion (chopped)
1	large green pepper (chopped)
2	T. oregano
3	bay leaves
3	medium potatoes (cubed)
3	T. flour
¼	c. water

Optional: 4 carrots (sliced)
1 — 1 lb. can string beans

1. Place olive oil in large, deep skillet or dutch oven along with meat, salt, pepper, garlic. Brown well.
2. Add tomatoes, onion and green pepper. Cook for few minutes longer.
3. Add oregano and bay leaves. Bring to boil.
4. Reduce heat to slow simmer. Cook for 30 minutes.
5. Add potatoes and cook until meat and potatoes are tender (about 30 minutes).
6. Mix flour and water together. Add to stew. Stir until thickened.

   *NOTE: If adding optional ingredients, add carrots with potatoes and add beans near end of cooking to heat through.

Serves: 4
Preparation: 15 minutes
Cooking: 1 hour 15 minutes

"Delicious served with hard rolls. Sop up the delectable juice. Serve with tossed green salad!"

SPANISH CREAM

1	qt. milk
⅛	t. salt
1	cinnamon stick
	rind of ¼-½ lemon (keep whole but do not get into the bitter white layer)
3	eggs
½	c. cornstarch
1	c. sugar
1	T. vanilla
2	drops yellow food coloring
	sugar for topping

1. Bring milk to a boil with salt, cinnamon, and lemon rind in large saucepan.
2. In another saucepan combine all other ingredients, except sugar for topping, and mix very, very well.
3. Take cinnamon stick and lemon rind out of milk.
4. Put egg mixture over low heat and let it heat up slightly. While stirring, slowly pour milk into eggs and continue to cook until thick and bubbly.
5. Pour into 9x11" cake pan. Sprinkle sugar over top and allow it to sink in. Chill.

Serves: 6-8
Preparation: 10 minutes
Cooking: 30 minutes

"This dish is especially attractive if the top is burned with a special instrument found in gourmet shops!"

— NOTES —

Mel's
Hot Dogs

— *Tampa* —

MEL'S HOT DOGS
TAMPA

MEL'S SPRITE® SANGRIA
(Allow Time To Soak Overnight)

3	liters red burgundy wine (use a good one!)
4	oz. orange juice (fresh, but may substitute frozen)
3	oz. lemon juice (fresh, but may substitute frozen)
¾	c. sugar
2	t. cinnamon (ground)
1	liter Sprite®

1. Mix all ingredients except Sprite® to form a concentrated mixture. Soak overnight.
2. To serve, mix ⅓ Sprite® to ⅔ of the concentrated mixture for each serving.
3. Garnish with sliced fruit.
4. Pour into large pitcher fill with ice and serve.

Serves: 12-8 oz. servings.
Preparation: When made ahead, 2 minutes.

You'll want to make this Sprite® away.''

— NOTES —

MEL'S SPECIAL HOT DOG BASKET

1   natural casing kosher hot dog
1   poppy seed hot dog bun (from bakery)
2   T. kosher sauerkraut
2   T. kosher relish
2   T. Bermuda onion (chopped)
1   t. mustard
1   kosher pickle, sliced lengthwise

1. Steam hot dog in covered container using a vegetable steamer or similar device.
2. Heat bun until steamy. Place hot dog in bun. Arrange garnishes on top.
3. Serve in basket with crispy french fries made from premium quality Idaho Potatoes, fried in all-vegetable shortening.

Serves: 1
Preparation: 10 minutes
Cooking time: 5 minutes

"Hot Dog!"

— NOTES —

MEL'S MOTHER'S COLE SLAW

1½ lb. purple cabbage
1   medium carrot (½ c. shredded)
1   c. mayonnaise
¼   c. white vinegar
1   T. sugar
1   t. celery seed
     seasoned salt to taste

1. Shred cabbage and carrot in shredder or food
    processor.
2. Mix juices and seasonings. Pour over cabbage and
    carrot. Mix well. Refrigerate for half-hour before
    serving.

Serves: 6-8
Preparation: 20 minutes
Chill: 30 minutes

"Vinegar gives the salad a nice tangy flavor!"

— NOTES —

The Rib Junction

— *Land O' Lakes* —

PICNIC BAKED BEANS

55 oz. can Bush's Best canned beans
1 small Spanish onion (diced)
¼ c. dark brown sugar
1-2 T. Gulden's brown mustard
2 T. molasses
1-2 T. soy sauce
2 T. Worcestershire sauce
½ c. pork butt or rib shavings

1. Combine all ingredients. Cook on top of stove in cast iron pot.
2. Cook on low heat for 2-3 hours.

Serves: 12-15
Preparation: 10 minutes
Cooking: 2-3 hours

"We reduced this down from 5 cases of beans... you'll love the down-home flavor."

— NOTES —

BARBECUED RIBS A LA JUNCTION
(Make Sauce Ahead — Start Grill)

4-6 lbs. loin pork or beef ribs
1 c. Hunt's ketchup
1 c. tomato sauce (Theresa's, if available)
½ c. water
1 T. soy sauce
2 T. Worcestershire sauce
² T. prepared mustard
½ t. powdered garlic
  tabasco to taste
¼ c. beer (warm, domestic)
  Option: cayenne pepper, homegrown peppers
1 bottle Wishbone salad dressing

— RIBS —

1. Place ribs on rack over barbecue pit 2 feet above heat so they won't char. Make certain the coals are very hot.
2. Turn ribs frequently to keep juices inside. Cook for approximately 45 minutes.

— SAUCE —

3. Combine all ingredients except beer. Mix in warm beer, just enough to percolate all ingredients.
4. Cook the sauce until hot over medium heat. Stir well.
5. Baste ribs with sauce last 15 minutes or add sauce after barbecuing.

VARIATIONS: To make a great hot sauce, add cayenne pepper and several types of home grown peppers.

Serves: 4-6
Preparation: 10 minutes
Cooking: 45 minutes

"One of the tastiest barbecue sauces you'll ever taste!"

Jack's Skyway Restaurant, St. Petersburg, Florida

Jack's Skyway Restaurant

— *St. Petersburg* —

CAROL'S FISHBURGERS

2-2½ lbs.	boneless and skinless fish
3	c. water
1	T. salt
¼	c. onion (minced)
¼	c. celery (minced)
¼	c. green pepper (minced)
½	c. mashed potatoes
1	egg (beaten)
¾	t. Worcestershire sauce
⅛	t. garlic powder
½	T. MSG
½-⅓	c. breading mix
	oil for frying
	bakery buns

1. Bring fish to boil in salted water. Simmer only 10 minutes. Drain off water just until fish is slightly moist.
2. Crumble fish. Mix with other ingredients. Use enough breading mix to hold ingredients together.
3. Make into patties, using about 4 oz. per patty, each about 4″ in size and ⅜-½″ thick.
4. If more have been made than are needed, freeze between sheets of waxed paper.
5. Lay the remaining patties on cookie sheet or similar tray. Freeze several hours until frozen.
6. Deep fat fry frozen patties until golden brown in oil heated to 350°F.
7. Drain on paper towels. Serve on bun with tartar sauce. (See recipe on page 87)

Serves: 5
Preparation: 15 minutes
Cooking: 10 minutes
Freeze: 2-3 hours

"Make up a batch to freeze and have on hand for when needed!"

JACK'S CHILI

1	lb. lean ground beef (or ground chuck)
¾	c. tomato juice
1	15 oz. can whole tomatoes (crush with hand)
1	15 oz. can dark red kidney beans
¼	c. onions (diced)
⅓	c. celery (diced)
1	t. Worcestershire sauce
1½	T. chili powder
⅓	T. garlic powder
⅓	t. pepper
½	t. salt
½	t. cumin
	Optional: tabasco

1. Cook meat over medium heat until brown and crumbly.
2. Remove from heat. Drain grease. Add all the remaining ingredients. Mix thoroughly.
3. Return to heat and bring to boil, stirring constantly. Lower heat and simmer for 3 hours, covered. Stir occasionally.
4. Tabasco can be added if "hot" is desired.
5. Any extra can be frozen if cooled first.

Serves: 4
Preparation: 15 minutes
Cooking: 3 hours 15 minutes

"A very satisfying dish!"

— NOTES —

JACK'S S.O.S.
(Creamed Sausage on Biscuits)

2   T. vegetable oil
½   lb. spicy sausage meat (can use mild or hot)
¾   c. all-purpose flour
1   qt. milk
¾   t. salt
     pepper and sage to taste

1. Heat oil in 2-quart saucepan. Add sausage in small pieces. Cook on medium heat with lid.
2. As meat cooks, break up into crumbly texture while stirring several times. Cook until dark brown. (Do not drain)
3. Add flour — a little at a time — thoroughly mixing after each addition. Cook and stir frequently for 6-10 minutes.
4. Meanwhile, in another saucepan, heat milk and salt until just starting to boil.
5. Add hot milk to sausage mixture, a little at a time, while stirring constantly with wire whisk.
6. Allow to thicken for 5-8 minutes. Taste and add desired seasonings.
7. Serve over biscuits or toast points.

Serves: 4
Preparation: 5 minutes
Cooking: 20-25 minutes

"An old southern favorite that is always good!"

— NOTES —

SLOPPY JACKS

1	lb. ground beef (or ground chuck)
½	c. onion (minced)
¼	c. celery (minced)
⅔	c. green pepper (minced)
1	c. catsup
¼	c. water
1	T. liquid mustard
¼	t. salt
¼	t. garlic powder
½	t. pepper
2	c. finely shredded cabbage (⅛-³⁄₁₆" thick)

1. Cook ground beef (or chuck) in large skillet. Break apart until fine and crumbly. Drain grease.
2. Add all other ingredients, except cabbage. Mix thoroughly. Bring to boil.
3. Add cabbage. Mix thoroughly. Simmer with lid for 25 minutes. Stir frequently.
4. If extra has been made, portion out and freeze.* Serve the remaining in bakery buns and enjoy!

*Note: If available, best to use microwave oven to heat the frozen portions — will not dry them out.

Serves: 4-5
Preparation: 15 minutes
Cooking: 35 minutes

"A most unusual nutritious and different lunch dish, especially for growing Jacks of all ages!"

— NOTES —

— NOTES —

El Cap Inn

— *St. Petersburg* —

CHICKEN CACCIATORA

4   T. butter
5   T. lard
2   whole cloves garlic (crushed)
4   chicken breast halves (or other chicken pieces)
½   c. sherry
    pinch sage
    salt and pepper to taste
2   *Finger Hot* peppers (cut in half lengthwise,
    remove seeds)
2   *Hung Waxed* peppers (cut in half lengthwise,
    remove seeds)
½   c. fresh parsley (chopped)

1. Melt butter and lard in large skillet. Add garlic. Dry
    chicken pieces with paper towels. Add to skillet.
2. Brown on each side. Add sherry. Turn heat down
    and place half of each type of pepper on each
    chicken piece.
3. Cover and simmer for 20-30 minutes.
4. Remove lid, cover top with fresh parsley and
    simmer for another 5-10 minutes.
5. Serve with white rice and fresh Italian bread to dip
    into sauce.

NOTE: IMMEDIATELY after handling the fresh peppers, wash hands with plenty of soap and water and do not touch hands to face, especially eyes.

According to Mary Jean, this is a great dish to create after preparing hundreds of hamburgers a day for their customers. This is an old family recipe and is served in the Bonfili home twice a week.

Serves: 4
Preparation: 10 minutes
Cooking: 30-45 minutes

"Spicy hot without having a sauce spooned over. Unusual!"

— NOTES —

THE EL CAP BURGER

1   lb. ground chuck (from corn-fed steer)
4   "good buns" (homemade or from bakery)
    salt and freshly ground black pepper
4   process cheese slices
4   large Ruskin* tomato slices (or other kind of hearty tomato)
4   Bermuda onion slices (*largest* you can find)
4   crisp, fresh lettuce leaves
    homemade ketchup
    *Great Florida tomatoes!

1. Hand-pack patties (4 to pound). Chill until firm.
2. Use an old, well seasoned grill or electric frying pan (the oldness and seasoned surface are the secrets to cloning their burger). If you have a dual heat control grill, heat one side to 385°F for the buns and the other side to 340°F for the patties.
3. Place fresh patties on grill and cook partially. Do not press down. Turn over, salt and pepper second side. Cook until medium rare.
4. Top with cheese slices, remove and place on bottom of grilled bun. Add tomato and onion slices and lettuce. Follow with top of grilled bun.

Variations: Add your favorite seasonings, if desired.

Serves: 4
Preparation: 15 minutes
Cooking: 5 minutes

"The finest ingredients make the finest meals!"

— NOTES —

Chris'
Restaurant

— *Fort Pierce* —

POTATO SOUP

3   **large white potatoes (peeled, cooked, diced)**
1   **stalk celery (diced)**
1   **carrot (diced)**
½   **small onion (diced)**
1   **T. pimiento**
1   **qt. milk**
       salt and pepper to taste
½   **c. fresh or frozen peas**
¼   **c. + 2 T. flour**
¼   **c. water**

1. Combine first six ingredients plus salt and pepper in large pot.
2. Cover. Simmer over low heat until vegetables are tender.
3. Approximately one-half hour prior to serving, add peas.
4. 5 minutes prior to serving, mix flour and water together to make a paste. Add to soup. Cook until thickened. Stir several times.

Serves: 6
Preparation: 20 minutes
Cooking: 45 minutes to 1 hour

"Great for a chilly night — warms you throughout!"

— NOTES —

CHRIS' SPECIALTY — LIVER AND ONIONS
(Freeze Liver Ahead)

1   lb. baby beef liver or calves liver (in slices)
½   c. flour
     vegetable oil (for frying)
2   large onions (sliced thin)
¼   c. butter

1. Freeze slices of liver singly. Thaw until hard but sliceable.
2. Cut in very, very thin slices (less than ¼ " thick) (devein and skin slices if necessary)
3. Gently dip into flour to seal juices.
4. Saute onions slowly, in butter, until almost transparent.
5. Heat thin layer of vegetable oil in another skillet to 350 °F.
6. Add floured liver to heated oil. Cook for **only** ½ minute on each side.
7. Serve liver with the sauteed onions.

Serves: 4
Preparation: Several hours to freeze liver plus
                20 minutes
Cooking: 15 minutes

"The secret to delicious liver is the short hot cooking — It's delicious!"

— NOTES —

RICE PUDDING

1 c. long grain white rice
2 c. water
½ t. salt
2 c. milk
1 c. sugar
2 large eggs
¼ t. cinnamon
Optional: Raisins

1. Combine rice, water, and salt in pan. Bring to boil. Simmer until tender and dry.
2. Add 1½ cups milk. Add sugar to rice.
3. Combine other ½ cup milk and eggs. Beat until smooth.
4. Temper egg mixture by adding a small amount of warmed milk from rice pan to bowl. (Bring eggs up to very warm temperature while stirring them.)
5. Slowly, and stirring constantly, pour tempered egg mixture back into rice pan. Cook over low heat until thick.
6. Add cinnamon.

Serves: 8
Preparation: 5 minutes
Cooking: 30 minutes

"Like momma used to make!! A thick pudding and excellent!"

— NOTES —

— NOTES —

The Desert Inn, Yeehaw Junction, Florida

P Stockey

The Desert Inn

— Yeehaw Junction —

POTATO SALAD

---

3   lbs. potatoes
2½ c. mayonnaise
¾   c. dill pickle relish
¼   c. pimiento
¼   c. onion (chopped)
¼   c. prepared mustard (brown will give a tasty zing)
    salt and pepper to taste
1   dozen cooked eggs (chopped)

1. Peel potatoes. Boil whole until done. Cool.
2. Cut into 1¼ " chunks. Place in large bowl.
3. Mix together all remaining ingredients except eggs. Stir into potatoes.
4. Add eggs to potatoes and mix gently. Chill until ready to serve.

Serves: 8-10
Preparation: 20 minutes
Cooking: 30 minutes
Chill: 2-4 hours

"Simple but more flavorful than most!"

— NOTES —

DESERT INN MEATLOAF

2   lbs. hamburger (best to use ground chuck or round)
2   eggs
2   hamburger buns (broken into small pieces)
½   c. onion (diced)
½   c. green pepper (diced)
¼   c. catsup
¼   c. sugar
    several dashes tabasco sauce
¼   c. yellow cornmeal
½   c. grated cheddar cheese
    salt and pepper to taste

1. In large mixing bowl, break apart meat. Add all remaining ingredients.
2. Using clean hands (minus any jewelry) squish all ingredients together until well mixed.
3. Form into loaf shape and place in 8 x 10" baking dish.
4. Bake in 300 °F oven for 1-1½ hours, until done.

Serves: 8
Preparation: 15 minutes
Cooking: 1-1½ hours

"Catsup and sugar blend together beautifully to form a glaze-like mixture. Your mouth will water for weeks."

— NOTES —

DESERT INN PECAN PIE

6   **eggs**
1   **c. sugar**
2   **T. melted butter**
2   **t. vanilla**
1   **T. flour**
1½ **c. maple syrup**
9½ -10" **deep dish unbaked pie shell**
    whole pecan halves

1. Whip eggs. Add sugar, mix well.
2. Add butter, vanilla, flour and maple syrup, blending well and until smooth.
3. Pour into pie shell. Place pecans in single layer in a circular pattern across top.
4. Bake at 400 °F for an additional 40 minutes.

Serves: 8
Preparation: 15 minutes
Cooking: 50 minutes

"Unusual variation, not as overbearingly rich as most pecan pies."

— NOTES —

The Crab Trap

— *Palmetto* —

CRAB TRAP FRITTERS

½   lb. blue crab meat (preferably fresh)
1   egg
¼   c. milk
1   c. all purpose biscuit mix
     juice of whole lemon
⅛   t. garlic salt
¼   t. salt
½   t. parsley flakes
6   drops Worcestershire sauce
     vegetable oil

1. **Carefully** remove all cartilage from crab meat.
2. In a bowl beat egg. Add milk and stir in biscuit mix.
3. Add seasonings and crab meat. Mix gently.
   Set aside.
4. In a very heavy skillet, heat 2 or 3 inches of oil to
   375°F.
5. Drop batter into hot oil by half teaspoonsful.
   Fry until golden brown.

Serves: 4-6
Preparation: 10 minutes
Cooking: 5-10 minutes

"Great with tartar sauce or cocktail sauce!"

— NOTES —

CRAB TRAP CRAB CREPES

— CREPE BATTER —

¾ c. sifted flour
½ t. salt
2 eggs (beaten)
1 c. milk
1 t. melted butter

— CREPE FILLING —

2 T. butter
2 T. flour
½ t. tabasco sauce
¼ t. Worcestershire sauce
½ t. dry mustard
½ t. salt
1 c. evaporated milk
2 T. Parmesan cheese
1 T. cream sherry wine
12 oz. blue crab meat (preferably fresh)

— CREPE BATTER —

1. Combine flour, salt, eggs and milk. Blend until smooth.
2. To mixture add melted butter and blend. Let stand several hours.
3. Heat a 5″ skillet. Using about 2 tablespoons crepe batter for each crepe, spread evenly by tilting pan. Brown crepe.
4. As each crepe is done, place in separate pan. Cover to keep warm.

— FILLING —

5. Melt butter. Add flour, tabasco, Worcestershire, mustard and salt. Blend slowly. Add evaporated milk. Stir until thick.
6. Remove from heat. Stir in Parmesan and cream sherry to make crepe sauce.

7. Add ¼ cup of crepe sauce to the crab meat (be sure to remove all cartilage) and mix.
8. Place 3 tablespoons or 1½ oz. of crab meat mixture into crepe. Gently roll up.
9. Place rolled crepe in shallow baking dish. Thin remaining sauce and gently spoon over crepes. Bake at 400°F for 10-12 minutes.

Serves: 4-6
Preparation: 2-3 hours for crepes to set
Cooking: 15 minutes crepes/20 minutes filling

"A very easy-no-fail recipe!"

— NOTES —

CHICKEN BALTIMORE

4   chicken breast halves (de-boned)
4   T. butter
    salt and pepper to taste
8   scalloped bananas (See recipe on page 65)
4   peach halves and juice

1. Saute chicken breasts in butter, salt, and pepper until tender and browned.
2. Serve each with 2 scalloped bananas alongside and a peach half and juice on top.

Serves: 4
Preparation: 10 minutes
Cooking: 15-20 minutes

"Pretty as a picture!"

— NOTES —

OYSTERS PARISIAN

½   c. butter
1   c. Parmesan cheese
½   c. cracker crumbs
1   t. dry mustard
    whole oysters (quantity depends on number
    to serve)
    sour cream

1. Soften butter. Combine cheese, crumbs and mustard.
2. Form into roll approximately 2½ " in diameter. Roll in waxed paper and chill until firm.
3. Shuck oysters. Leave in half shell. Top each with 1 t. sour cream and slice of Parmesan/butter roll.
4. Bake in 350°F oven until golden brown, about 10-12 minutes.

Serves: you decide
Preparation: 1 hour 25 minutes
Cooking: 15 minutes

"What could be easier if oysters are shucked ahead of time!"

— NOTES —

SCALLOPED BANANAS

4	medium ripe bananas
1	c. flour
½	c. milk
1	c. bread crumbs (unseasoned)
	oil for frying
⅓	c. cinnamon/sugar mixture (equal mix)

1. Cut bananas into 3-4 1¾" chunks.
2. Roll each chunk in flour. Dip in milk, then roll in bread crumbs.
3. Deep fat fry in oil heated to 350°F until golden.
4. Roll in cinnamon/sugar mixture. Serve warm.

Serves: 4-6
Preparation: 10 minutes
Cooking: 5 minutes

"Can be served as a side dish with meal or as a dessert. Either way is sure to please!"

— NOTES —

45

— NOTES —

Old Towne Cafe

— *Naples* —

CREAM OF MUSHROOM SOUP

3 T. butter
1 lb. large, fresh mushrooms (sliced)
1 t. fresh garlic (minced, in jar)
2 c. beef stock (best if homemade but may substitute canned bouillon or consomme)
2 c. milk
¼ c. butter (melted)
½ c. flour

1. Saute butter, mushrooms and garlic in large flat pan for several minutes.
2. Add beef stock. Boil mushrooms until dark brown (about 30 minutes).
3. Place mushroom mixture in double boiler. Add milk. Combine butter and flour in custard cup. Stir into a paste and then add a small amount of this mixture — a little at a time — to the double boiler. Stir well.
4. Simmer until thick (about 30 minutes). Stir often.

Serves: 4-6
Preparation: 10 minutes
Cooking: 1 hour

"Almost thick and rich enough to slice!"

— NOTES —

HOME FRIES

4	white idaho potatoes (washed)
1¾	c. chicken broth
8	slices bacon (each piece quartered)
2	medium onions (cut in 1″ chunks)
1	t. paprika

1. Cook potatoes (with skins on) in chicken broth until done. Place in refrigerator and cool for several hours.
2. Cut chilled potatoes in 1¼″ chunks.
3. Cook bacon until partially done. Then add onions and potatoes and brown nicely. Add paprika.

Serves: 4
Preparation: 15 minutes
Cooking: 20/10 minutes
Chill: 2 hours

*"I never knew potatoes could taste this fabulous...
make plenty!"*

— NOTES —

GENTLEMAN'S TOAST
(Herron Toast)

2	slices buffet ham
2	slices vienna or french bread
1-2	slices tomato
	garlic salt
	oregano
1	slice Swiss cheese
1	egg (beaten)

1. Saute ham slices, briefly. Place on 1 slice of bread.
2. Place tomato on ham. Sprinkle garlic and oregano over. Top with Swiss cheese and other slice of bread.
3. Dip the whole sandwich in egg and water.
4. Fry in pan on both sides until golden.

Serves: 1
Preparation: 5 minutes
Cooking: 5 minutes

"A nice hot sandwich for lunch — serve with gelatin salad!"

— NOTES —

Timmy's Nook

— *Captiva Island* —

QUICK CORN CHOWDER

2 c. whole kernel corn
3 slices bacon (cooked crisp and crumbled)
1 T. bacon drippings
1 c. cooked potatoes (diced)
¼ c. onion (minced)
1½ cans Legout mushroom soup (may substitute
Campbell's Golden Mushroom Soup)
2 T. chopped pimiento
1½-2 c. real thick chicken broth
(suggestion: 12 oz. jar Heinz Home Chicken Gravy)
½ c. butter
beau monde seasoning to taste
white pepper to taste
dash marjoram

1. Combine all ingredients in large saucepan.
2. Heat to boiling and then simmer for 15 minutes.
3. Serve hot.

Serves: 4
Preparation: 20 minutes
Cooking: 20 minutes

"So rich, so thick, soooo... GOOD!"

— NOTES —

CRAB MEAT STUFFING

¾ c. water
½ c. butter
¼ c. white wine (chablis)
2 T. cooking sherry
½ t. white pepper
1½ t. salt
1 large onion (diced)
1 large green pepper (diced)
½ stalk celery (diced)
3 oz. milk (or half-n-half)
½ lb. snow crab crab meat
3 T. cornstarch
1 T. water
1 c. bread crumbs

1. Place first six ingredients in pot. Bring to boil. Add onion, green pepper and celery.
2. Return to boil and cook al dente. Add milk and crab meat.
3. Combine cornstarch and water in custard cup. Add to pot and cook until the consistency of wallpaper paste.
4. Reduce heat. Simmer for 5 minutes. Remove from heat. Add bread crumbs and stir well.
5. Fill split jumbo shrimp, flounder fillets, or crepes with stuffing.

Yield: 4 cups
Preparation: 20 minutes
Cooking: 15/10/5 minutes

"Adds a new dimension to fish, shrimp or crepes and easy to prepare."

CRAB MEAT CREPES WITH LEMON CHEESE SAUCE

— CREPE BATTER —

2	eggs
⅛	t. salt
1	c. flour
1	c. milk
¼	c. melted butter
	oil for frying

— LEMON CHEESE SAUCE —

¾	c. water
1	c. butter
1	t. salt
¼	t. white pepper
4	slices process Swiss cheese, cut in squares
2	T. cornstarch
1	T. water
2	T. lemon juice
¼	c. half-n-half

— CRAB MEAT STUFFING —
(See recipe on page 77)

— CREPES —

1. Combine eggs, salt, flour, milk and melted butter in mixing bowl. Beat for several minutes (or in blender for 1 minute).
2. Refrigerate for at least 1 hour before making up crepes.
3. Place a small amount of oil in bottom of 7½" or 9" fry pan. Add 2-3 T. batter and cook until done and lightly browned on one side.
   NOTE: Crepes can be made ahead and stored in refrigerator or freezer with layer of waxed paper between each crepe. Warm crepes before serving.

— LEMON CHEESE SAUCE —

4. Boil water, butter, salt and white pepper in pan.
5. Add Swiss cheese and stir until melted.

6. Place cornstarch and water into custard cup, blend together and add to sauce in pot.
7. Stir to thicken several minutes. Add lemon juice and half-n-half.
8. Take 1 crepe and place on plate with non-browned side up. Add 1 large spoonful of crab meat stuffing along center of crepe. Fold ends over the filling.
9. Top crepes with hot cheese sauce and serve.

Serves: 6
Preparation: 30 minutes
Cooking: 10 minutes (sauce)
          20 minutes (crepes)

"Much of this can be prepared ahead of time — great for a dinner party!"

— NOTES —

BLUEBERRY SOUR CREAM PIE

1   c. sugar
½ t. salt
¼ c. flour
2   eggs
2   c. sour cream
¾ t. almond extract
1   unbaked 9" graham cracker pie shell
1   can blueberry pie filling

1. In mixing bowl combine all ingredients except pie shell and pie filling. Mix well.
2. Pour into pie shell and bake in 350°F. oven for 30 minutes or until center is set.
3. Top hot pie with blueberries. Chill several hours.
4. When ready to serve, top with Cool Whip or whipped cream.

Serves: 8
Preparation: 5 minutes
Cooking: 30 minutes
Chill: 2-3 hours

"Elegant looking... but easy!"

— NOTES —

— NOTES —

The Snook Inn, Matlacha, Florida

Snook Inn

— *Matlacha* —

OYSTER SANDWICH

1   large, whole oyster (fresh or canned)
1 can beer (domestic will do fine)
2   T. buttermilk pancake mix
peanut oil (for frying)
large bakery bun, grilled
Swiss cheese slice
tartar or cocktail sauce (best to use a *great* tartar sauce) (See recipe on page 87)

1. Take 1 oyster, dipping first in beer then in pancake mix. Deep fat fry in peanut oil which has been heated to 375 °F.
2. Fry until oyster floats. Place on bun.
3. Place slice of Swiss cheese over top of oyster allowing heat from oyster to melt it.
4. Serve with tartar or cocktail sauce as preferred.

Serves: 1 sandwich per person
Preparation: 10 minutes
Cooking: 3-5 minutes per sandwich

"Oyster Heaven"

— NOTES —

TARTAR SAUCE

1   c. salad dressing
¼   c. dill relish
½   T. brown mustard (French's Bold & Spicy)

1. Combine the salad dressing, dill relish, and brown mustard. Mix well.
2. Refrigerate until needed.

Yield: 1 cup

"Simply Delicious"

— NOTES —

FRIED GROUPER

1   lb. grouper fillets (prefer fresh)
1   small can beer
1   c. buttermilk pancake mix (not the complete mix variety)
    peanut oil (for frying)

1. Cut fillets into fingers (about 1″ wide and 5″ long.)
2. Dip fingers into beer. Roll in pancake mix.
3. Heat peanut oil to 375 °F in deep fat fryer or pan with wire basket.
4. Drop freshly coated fingers into heated peanut oil. Cook for 3-4 minutes, until they float to the top and the outside darkens.
5. Serve with Snook Inn Tartar Sauce.
   (Recipe on page 87.)

Serves: 2
Preparation: 10 minutes
Cooking: 10 minutes

"Despite its simplicity, everyone will ask how you make this dish!"

— NOTES —

SNOOK INN CRAB CAKES

2 c. water
2 c. instant mashed potatoes
2 T. butter
1 lb. crab meat (fresh or canned)
¼ c. minced onion
1 T. plus 1 t. mayonnaise
1¼ t. salt
1¼ t. Old Bay seasoning
1 T. Worcestershire sauce
1 T. baking powder
1 whole egg plus 1 egg white
  peanut oil (for frying)
  Snook Inn tartar sauce (See recipe on page 87)

1. Heat water to boiling. Add potatoes and butter. Mix well and let cool in refrigerator until crab is fixed.
2. Thoroughly rinse and drain crab meat. Using fingers, check through meat and remove any remaining pieces of shell or cartilage.
3. Combine cooled potatoes, crab meat, and onion. Mix until well blended.
4. Add remaining ingredients (except peanut oil). Mix well. Return to refrigerator. Chill for 3-4 hours.
5. Heat peanut oil to 375°F. Make crab mixture into patties slightly smaller than desired cooked patty (they puff!)
6. Cook patties until golden brown on both sides. They float on top. Serve with a good tartar sauce. (See recipe on page 87)

Serves: 6
Preparation: 30 minutes
Chill: 3-4 hours
Cooking: 10 minutes

"For an interesting luncheon dish serve on grilled bakery buns."

— NOTES —

State Farmers Market Restaurant

— *Fort Myers* —

DEEP FRIED CHICKEN LIVERS

1   lb. chicken livers*
1   c. milk
3   raw eggs
1   T. salt
1   T. black pepper
1   T. Vegit® (may substitute Spike seasoning)— Both
    can be found in any health food store)
½-1 c. flour
    oil for frying

1. Cut apart chicken livers if joined by membrane
    (you want individual livers).
2. Combine milk, eggs, salt, pepper, and Vegit® in
    bowl. Blend mixture with wire wisp.
3. Dip livers in egg batter and then into small amount
    of flour.
4. Heat oil in deep fat fryer to 375°F. Cook livers 'til
    golden brown (about 5 minutes). Serve hot.

Serves: 6 as a main dish or 20-25 appetizers
Preparation: 5 minutes
Cooking: 15 minutes

"These are delicious — even for non-liver lovers!"

*NOTE: Substitute gizzards for livers if you desire or
    use a combination of the two.

— NOTES —

CHICKEN WITH YELLOW RICE PILAF

1	3 lb. fryer chicken, cut up
2	c. cold water
1	T. yellow food coloring
½	c. celery (diced)
½	c. cup green pepper (diced)
½	c. onion (diced)
1	t. Accent
½	t. black pepper
2	chicken bouillon cubes
1	c. long grain raw rice

1. Place chicken, water, and food coloring in large saucepan. Stir.
2. Add the remaining ingredients except rice. Stir to mix well.
3. Cover and cook for 45 minutes to 1 hour or until chicken is almost done.
4. Add rice. Cover and cook until rice is partially cooked. Remove lid and finish cooking until rice is cooked and dry.
5. Serve. Excellent with tossed salad or fruited gelatin salad.

Serves: 3-4
Preparation: 10 minutes
Cooking: 1½ hours

"An easy dish to prepare with a great blending of flavors!"

— NOTES —

TURNIP GREENS WITH ROOTS

---

1   **box turnip greens with chopped pieces (frozen)**
½   **c. salt pork (diced)**
1½ **c. cold water**
½   **c. margarine**
     salt and pepper to taste

1. Place greens in shallow 2-quart pot. Add salt pork and water.
2. Bring to boil. Simmer for 1 hour.
3. Add margarine. Cook for 15 minutes.
4. Salt and pepper to taste.

Serves: 3-4
Preparation: 5 minutes
Cooking: 1 hour

"A good southern favorite that is easy to prepare!"

— NOTES —

SPICED APPLES

1	**16 or 20 oz. can sliced apples**
¾	**c. granulated sugar**
1	**t. nutmeg**
1	**t. cinnamon**
1	**t. allspice**
1	**T. imitation vanilla flavoring (can also use vanilla extract)**
1	**c. cold water**

1. Drain apples and place in shallow baking pan.
2. Combine all other ingredients. Mix well with apples.
3. Cover pan with aluminum foil and bake in 375°F oven for 45 minutes.
4. Serve hot.

Serving Suggestions: Serve over Vanilla Pudding, Tapioca or Ice Cream!

Serves: 4
Preparation: 5 minutes
Cooking: 45 minutes

"Easy... could be the spice of life!"

— NOTES —

Flora & Ella's Restaurant, LaBelle, Florida

Flora
and Ella's
Restaurant

— *LaBelle* —

FRESH COCONUT CAKE

1   box cake mix (white, yellow or chocolate)
16 oz. coconut (frozen or canned moist)
16 oz. sour cream
2   c. sugar
9   oz. whipped topping (Cool Whip)

1. Prepare cake mix according to directions baking in 3-9" layers (it will take less time than directions say so watch carefully 10 minutes before end of baking time).
2. Combine coconut, sour cream and sugar. Let stand 2 hours.
3. After cake has cooled place one layer on serving plate.
4. Reserve one-half cup of coconut mixture for topping on bottom layer.
5. Place second layer on top and use remaining half of coconut mixture to cover. Follow with third layer.
6. Mix the one-half cup reserved coconut mixture together with whipped topping. Frost top and sides of cake with it.
7. Refrigerate for 2 days before serving.

Yield: 1-9" cake
Preparation: 20 minutes
Cooking: 25 minutes
Chill: 2 days

"If you can manage to keep little fingers out of the cake until it's set — the wait is worth it!"

— NOTES —

SWAMP CABBAGE SALAD

1   head lettuce, torn into bite-size pieces
1   avocado
2   c. raw swamp cabbage* (soak in strong salt water
     20 minutes and drain) (May substitute 2 large cans
     of Hearts of Palm, found in Gourmet Specialty
     Shops and Supermarkets.)
     French dressing
     salt and lots of pepper to taste
     *Also known as Sabal Palm

1. Gently toss salad ingredients. Add French
   dressing. Toss again.
2. Salt and pepper to taste.

    *Note: At this time the Sabal Palm is not a state
    protected species. However, many counties
    in Florida regulate and protect the species.
    If you desire the raw cabbage, be sure to
    call your local county government and ask
    for local regulations regarding the palm.

Serves: 4-6
Preparation: 20 minutes soak/5 minutes

"A refreshing salad on a hot summer's day!"

— NOTES —

SWAMP CABBAGE WITH TOMATOES

½   c. salt pork or slab bacon (diced)
½   c. onions (diced)
1   14 oz. can swamp "cabbage" (Hearts of Palm)
1   16 oz. can sliced stewed tomatoes
     salt and pepper to taste

1.   Place salt pork or slab bacon in 2-quart saucepan and cook for a few minutes over low heat.
2.   Add onion to pan and saute until onion is slightly browned and transparent.
3.   Slice swamp cabbage across the stalks into ¼-½" slices. Add to saucepan.
4.   Add the remaining ingredients and mix well. Cook until cabbage is done, about 10-15 minutes.

Serves: 4
Preparation: 5 minutes
Cooking: 20-25 minutes

"A delicious vegetable to serve with fish, meat, or poultry."

— NOTES —

SWAMP CABBAGE PATTIES

2   c. cooked swamp cabbage* (drained — may substitute 2 cans Hearts of Palm, found in Gourmet Specialty Shops and Supermarkets)
1   c. water
½   c. onion (finely chopped)
1   egg (slightly beaten)
    salt and lots of pepper to taste
    flour
    bacon fat or cooking oil

1. Cook swamp cabbage partially in water. Be sure to cook with lots of pepper.
2. Remove from pot and dice. Combine with onion, egg, salt, and pepper. Add flour a little at a time until stiff.
3. Heat griddle or frying pan with 1" fat in bottom. Drop mixture by teaspoon into hot grease. Fry until brown. Serve hot.

*Note: In the matter of black pepper in swamp cabbage we must refer to Mark Twain's statement pertaining to the amount of Bourbon to put in egg nog, "Too much is exactly enough." Regardless of the amount used, it is essential that the pepper be cooked with the cabbage.

Serves: 6
Preparation: 10 minutes
Cooking: 10 minutes

"You'll be swamped with extra dinner guests after this one!"

CHICKEN WITH DUMPLINGS

1	large chicken (about 3-3½ lbs.) (cleaned)
1-1½ qts. water
1	small onion (chopped)
2	stalks celery (chopped)
1	t. salt
1	t. black pepper
1	c. flour
	pinch baking powder
1	large egg
¼-⅓	c. chicken broth
	salt and pepper to taste

1. In large pot place chicken, water, onion, celery, salt, and pepper.
2. Cook chicken until done. Remove from broth and allow to cool.
3. In bowl place flour and baking powder. Make deep well in center. Add egg and chicken broth.
4. Gently beat egg and broth together. Mix in surrounding flour. Form into ball.
5. Pinch small amount of dough and roll on floured board. Roll **very thin**.
6. Cut into ½" strips and drop into boiling chicken broth. Cook slowly until tender.
7. Meanwhile, pick meat from chicken. Cut into bite-size pieces and return to pot with dumplings once they are tender.
8. Heat through and thicken with flour if necessary.

Serves: 6
Preparation: 20 minutes
Cooking: 40 minutes

"Good down-home stick-to-the-rib cookin'!"

CORNMEAL MUFFINS

1   c. flour
1   c. cornmeal
¼   c. sugar
¼   t. salt
4   t. baking powder
    pinch baking soda
2   large eggs
1   c. buttermilk
⅓   c. melted butter

1. Mix flour, cornmeal, sugar, salt, baking powder, and baking soda.
2. Add eggs, buttermilk, and butter. Blend until just moistened. (Do not overmix.)
3. Grease 18-cup muffin pans (or use non-stick pan). Fill cups three-quarters full.
4. Bake in 425°F oven about 10 minutes.

Yield: 18
Preparation: 10 minutes
Cooking: 10 minutes

"An old Southern favorite!"

— NOTES —

PEAS AND RICE

— RICE —

1	c. rice (long-grain white)
2	c. water
2	t. salt
2	T. butter

— PEAS —

2	c. water
1	lb. fresh blackeyed peas (may substitute frozen)
¼	lb. salt pork (diced)
1	small onion (finely chopped)

1. Wash rice in water. In heavy pot combine rice, water, salt and butter. Cover.
2. Bring to boil, then simmer until dry. Do not stir.

— PEAS —

3. Bring the water to a boil. Add peas and salt pork. Cook until tender (45 minutes-1 hour).
4. Serve rice in an attractive bowl. Top with peas and "pot liquor" (juice from bottom). Sprinkle chopped onions over all. Enjoy.

Serves: 4
Preparation: 5 minutes
Cooking: 20 minutes/1 hour

"With corn meal muffins and butter, what a meal!"

— NOTES —

Ye Tower Lunch

— *Lantana* —

OLD FASHION MALTS

2 **ample scoops vanilla ice cream**
½ **c. milk**
1½ **T. malted milk**
1½ **oz. (scant ¼ c.) chocolate syrup**

1. Combine all ingredients in blender. Mix for just 5 seconds.
2. Pour into soda glass. Serve immediately. (If desired garnish with dolup of whipped cream and cherry)

Serves: 1
Preparation: 5 seconds

"For kids only, or adults young at heart."

— NOTES —

CORNED BEEF HASH

3	T. bacon fat (or use Crisco)
1	lb. can corned beef
3	potatoes (boiled, peeled, and sliced into flat walnut-size pieces)*
1	large onion (diced)
	salt & pepper
	Optional: 4 poached eggs

1. Heat fat in skillet (A preseasoned cast iron skillet works best.)
2. Add corned beef (broken into small pieces), potatoes, and onions.
3. Season with salt and pepper. Fry until brown.
4. Each serving may be served with optional poached egg placed on top.

*Boil potatoes with skins on until done. Place in refrigerator and when ready to use, take out ahead of time. Inside moisture will cause skins to separate from potatoes and come out of jackets easily.

Serves: 4
Preparation: 15 minutes
Cooking: 15 minutes

"A quick and filling lunch dish for the hearty appetite!"

— NOTES —

Sage Bagel & Appetizer Shop

Sage Bagel and Appetizer Shop

— *Hallandale* —

CHOPPED LIVER

1½ lb. **mild sweet onions, Bermuda or Spanish (chopped)**
½ lb. **chicken livers**
4 **hard boiled eggs**
1 c. **vegetable oil**
salt and pepper to taste

1. Saute liver and onions til brown, mixing thoroughly.
2. Combine liver, onions and eggs in food processor or blender.
3. Mix until mixture is of spreading consistency.
4. Add salt and white pepper to taste.
5. Serve on party rye, crackers, bagels, or stuff into celery or as an appetizer, garnished.

Makes: 3-4 cups
Preparation: 15-20 minutes
Chill: ½ hour

"A delicious blending of flavors — Make plenty — It will go fast!"

— NOTES —

VEGETABLE CREAM CHEESE

1 **c. minced fresh vegetables (even amounts of green pepper, peeled cucumbers, radishes, scallions, shredded carrots)**
2½ **8 oz. pkg. cream cheese, softened**

1. Mix vegetables and cream cheese together well.
2. Chill or serve immediately.

   *NOTE: Spread on snack breads, bagels, or crackers.

Makes: 3-4 cups
Preparation: 20 minutes
Chill: 1-2 hours

"Luscious especially when you have access to variety of fresh vegetables. Delicious to snack on and very nutritious too!"

— NOTES —

MUSHROOM AND EGG SALAD BAGEL SANDWICH

½   **lbs. mushrooms (chopped)**
2   **lbs. onions (chopped)**
10 **boiled and peeled eggs**
½   **c. Matzo meal**
1   **c. vegetable oil**
    salt and white pepper

1. Saute mushrooms and onions in vegetable oil until brown. BE CAREFUL NOT TO BURN.
2. Chop eggs and place in food processor.
3. Grind all ingredients together until chunky (not pureed).
4. Add Matzo meal, salt, and pepper.
5. Spread on bagel or crackers or serve as an appetizer, garnished.

Makes: 3-4 cups
Preparation: 15-20 minutes
Cooking: ½ hour

"A nutritious luncheon or snack dish!"

— NOTES —

Bimini Sea Shack

— *Ft. Lauderdale* —

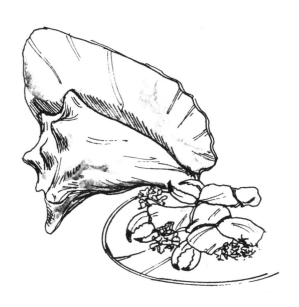

BIMINI BREAD

3	cakes yeast
¾	c. powdered dry milk
1	c. sugar
¾	c. oil
½	t. salt
3	eggs
2½	c. warm water
5	pounds all-purpose flour (sifted)

1. Using food processor, mixer, or hand, beat together yeast, dry milk, sugar, oil, salt, eggs, and ½ c. warm water.
2. In large pan pour the above ingredients. Add 2 c. warm water and slowly add the flour, several cups at a time, stirring well after each addition.
3. Knead in bowl. Let rise until double.
4. Place on large floured board. Knead until all air is out.
5. Cut into 7 pieces.
6. Place in buttered loaf pans or large cake pans.
7. Let loaves rise until double. Bake 30 minutes in 350°F oven.
8. Freeze extra loaves when cooled for future use.

Makes: 7 loaves
Preparation: 3-4 hours
Cooking: 30 minutes

"We have not reduced this recipe from the original. By using this exact recipe — unaltered — you will achieve the perfect results as experienced at the Bimini. Make this full recipe and always have homemade bread on hand!"

— NOTES —

BANANA DUFF

½ c. butter
½ c. sugar
2 eggs
2 c. flour
1 t. baking powder
¾ c. milk
bananas (cut in 1-2" pieces)
flour
water

1. Cream butter and sugar together. Add eggs and beat thoroughly.
2. Sift flour and baking powder together. Add alternately to creamed mixture along with milk. Form into ball.
3. Place flour on counter or board. Roll out dough as you would a pie crust. Cut into sections and roll around banana pieces.
4. Cook in water on top of double boiler until dough is done.

Makes: 1-2 dozen
Preparation: 10 minutes
Cooking: 10-15 minutes

"Serve as a side dish with entree or sprinkle with cinnamon-sugar mixture!"

— NOTES —

BIMINI KEY LIME PIE

1   can sweetened condensed milk
1   8 oz. pkg. cream cheese, softened
½-¾ c. juice from Key Limes (other limes will do, but
      not as tasty)
½   t. vanilla
1   9″ graham cracker pie crust
     Whipped cream topping

1. Combine milk, cream cheese, and lime juice in blender. Blend on low speed until smooth.
2. Add vanilla and stir into mixture.
3. Pour into graham cracker crust.
4. Chill in refrigerator until set.
5. Top with whipped cream before serving.

Serves: 8
Preparation: 5 minutes
Chill: 3-4 hours

"Perfect blending of flavors and so easy!"

— NOTES —

— NOTES —

Lime Tree Bay Cafe, Long Key, Florida

The Lime Tree Bay Cafe

— *Long Key* —

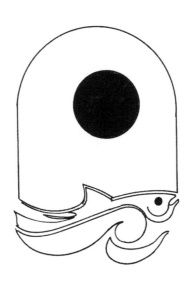

KEY LIME STRAWBERRY PINEAPPLE SHERBET

2   qts. whole milk
4½ c. sugar
1   fresh pineapple (cut into very small chunks)
1   pt. strawberries (cut into very small chunks)
     juice from 18 Key Limes (may substitute
     6 northern limes)
     juice from 2 oranges
     juice from 2 lemons
     grated rind from 3 Key Limes (may substitute
     1 northern lime)
     garnish of orange and lemon rind
     slices of lime
     Optional: whipped cream

1. Mix milk and sugar well. Place in shallow dish. Put into freezer until ice forms on top (the semi-frozen stage).
2. Meanwhile, mix pineapple, strawberries, various juices, and rind from 3 limes in bowl. Stir several times while standing.
3. When milk mixture is ready, add fruit. Mix well. Return to freezer.
4. Serve when not quite frozen (The consistency of soft-serve ice cream).
5. Garnish with grated orange and lemon rind and a slice of lime. Whipped cream on top is optional!

NOTE: Leftover sherbet can be kept well in freezer. It will freeze solid but when some is needed, allow to stand at room temperature until softened.

Makes: ½ gallon
Preparation: 30 minutes
Freezing: 2-3 hours for both steps

"A fabulous dessert with a tangy taste that sits well after a hearty meal!"

FISH ESCOVITCH

4   fish fillets (grouper or snapper)
1   c. mayonnaise
2   T. horseradish
1   T. lemon juice (fresh squeezed)
2   pinches Old Bay seasoning
½   c. green pepper (diced)
½   c. onion (diced)
½   c. tomato (diced)

1.   Place fish in single layer into shallow baking dish.
2.   Mix together mayonnaise, horseradish, lemon juice, and Old Bay seasoning. Pour over top of fish.
3.   Bake in oven at 400°F for 8-12 minutes, longer depending on thickness of fish.
4.   Place raw green pepper, onion, and tomato over top of sauce. Place under broiler for several minutes, until golden brown.

Serves: 4
Preparation: 5 minutes
Cooking: 15 minutes

"A refreshing way to serve fish!"

— NOTES —

LIME TREE BAY CAFE
KEY WEST

FISH ALMONDINE

4 **fillets (use grouper, snapper, or even dolphin)**
1 **egg (beaten)**
1 **c. prepared bread crumbs**
butter for frying
¾ **c. sliced blanched almonds (can use 'slivered' but not as colorful as 'sliced')**
fresh chopped parsley (garnish)
juice of ½ lemon (garnish)

1. Dip fillets in beaten egg. Then dip into bread crumbs.
2. Heat butter in saute or frying pan,* add fillets. Cook until edges are brown.
3. Pour off butter. Cover fillets with almonds.
4. Bake in 400°F oven until you can smell the almonds — approximately 5 minutes baking time.
5. Top with parsley and lemon juice.

*Use pan that is oven-proof, or remove handle.

Serves: 4
Preparation: 5 minutes
Cooking: 10-15 minutes

"The almonds give the fish a delightful taste and crunchy texture!"

— NOTES —

Capt. Bobs
Shrimp Dock

— *Key West* —

CONCH CHOWDER

⅓   c. onion (diced)
2   T. cooking oil
3   1 lb. cans potatoes (drained and diced)
2   t. Kitchen Bouquet
2   t. oregano
1   t. black pepper
2   t. salt
1   bay leaf
2   t. Accent
½   t. garlic powder
2½ lbs. conch (or may substitute clams. In Florida, purchase conch at your local seafood market.*)
3-4 stalks celery
1-2 large carrots
⅓   c. tomato paste
¼   c. green pepper (diced)
3-4 qts. water

1. In large pot saute onion in oil. Add potatoes and seasonings.
2. Grind conch, celery, and carrots until fine. Add to pot along with tomato paste and green pepper.
3. Add 3-4 quarts water. Cook over medium-low heat for 4-5 hours (if using clams grind them alone and add 1 hour before serving).
4. Serve or cool if you have extra. (Make sure the soup is cool before refrigeration, otherwise the conch will sour.)

    *If you'd like the name of a supplier from whom you can purchase conch, write us and we'll gladly furnish you with a list of suppliers.

Makes: 1½ gallons
Preparation: 20 minutes
Cooking: 5 hours

"A delicious blend of flavors causing aromas that will make your mouth water while it's cooking!"

98

CONCH FRITTERS

3	c. water
1	t. Accent
½	t. garlic powder
1	t. salt
½	t. black pepper
¾	t. oregano
4-6	c. self-rising flour
1	lb. conch meat (fresh ground or frozen — may substitute clams)
½	c. green pepper (diced)
	oil for frying

1. Mix water and spices together.
2. Add flour until drop consistency.
3. Add remaining ingredients.
4. Batter should be stiff enough to drop by teaspoon into oil heated to 350°F. Cook until brown.

Makes: 8-10 dozen
Preparation: 15 minutes
Cooking: 15-25 minutes

*"A pleasant delight to your taste buds.
You'll love conch!"*

— NOTES —

REAL KEY LIME PIE

5   egg yolks
1   can sweetened condensed milk
5   oz. (scant ⅔ c.) Key Lime juice
    graham cracker crust
    meringue or whipped cream, optional

1. In bowl blend egg yolks and milk.
2. Add lime juice — quickly while stirring.
3. Pour into crust.
4. Chill.
5. Add toppings, if desired.
    NOTE: If unable to get Key Lime juice use equal
          amounts of juice from fresh limes and
          lemons. Do **NOT** use bottled juice.

Serves: 6-8
Preparation: 5 minutes
Chill: 2-3 hours

"The world famous pie — straight from the area it was named for!"

— NOTES —

Lunch
on Limoges

— *Dade City* —

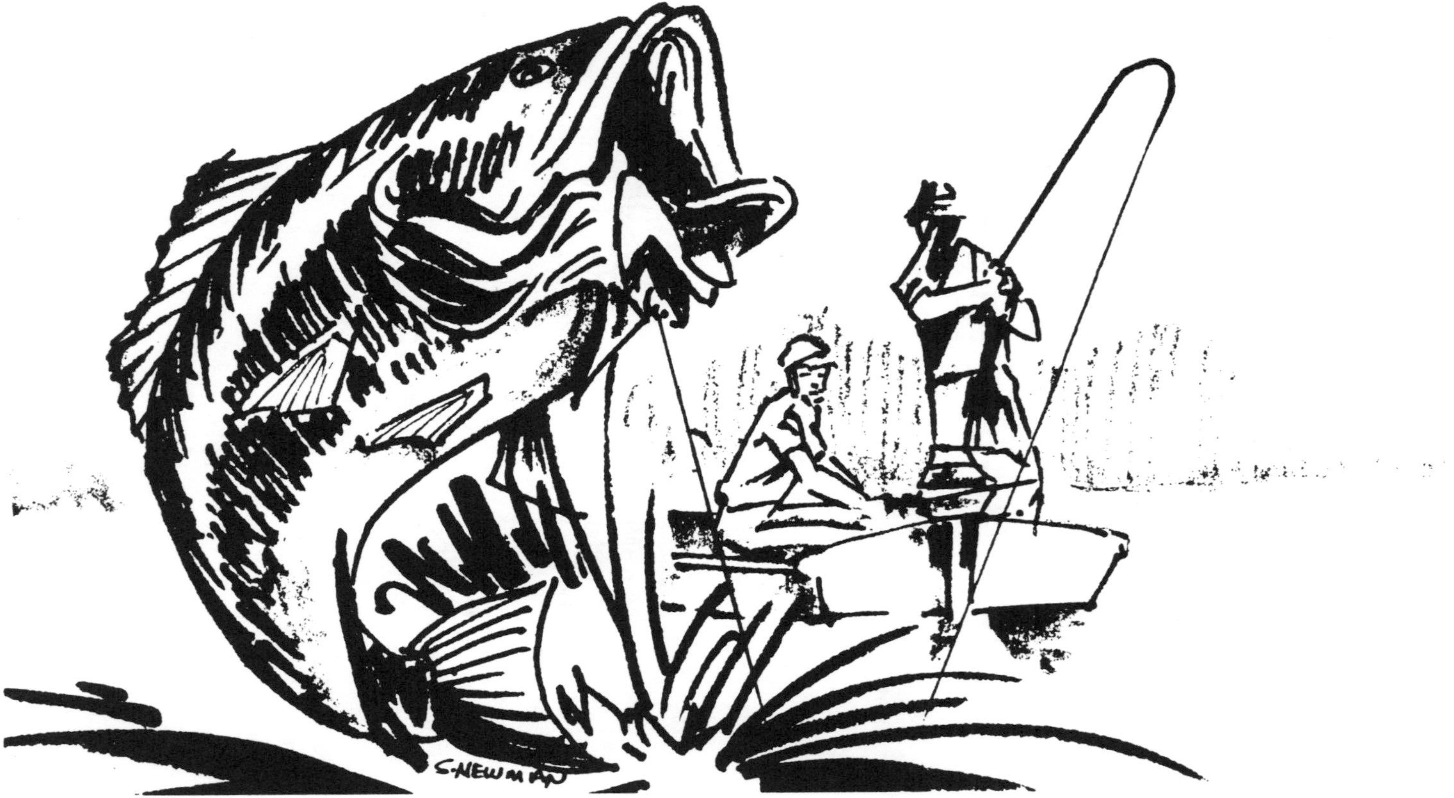

Fishing on Orange Lake, Cross Creek

BROCCOLI MUSHROOM SOUP

1   c. leeks (sliced)
1   c. mushrooms (sliced)
3   T. butter
¼   c. flour
3   c. chicken broth
1   c. broccoli florets (chopped)
1   c. light cream
1   c. Swiss cheese (shredded)
2   eggs

1. In large saucepan, place leeks, mushrooms, and butter. Saute until tender (do not brown).
2. Add flour and stir until bubbly.
3. Remove from heat and gradually add chicken broth, stirring until mixed.
4. Return to heat and cook still stirring until thickened and smooth.
5. Add broccoli. Reduce. Simmer 15 minutes or until vegetables are tender.
6. Mix cream, Swiss cheese, and eggs in mixing bowl. Temper by adding a small amount of soup to the bowl until ingredients are warm, stirring constantly.
7. While stirring, slowly pour the tempered egg mixture into pot.
8. Simmer until heated through and cheese is thoroughly melted.

Serves: 8
Preparation: 15 minutes
Cooking: 35 minutes

"A delightful blending of flavors!"

POPPY SEED DRESSING

¾ c. sugar
1 c. vegetable oil
⅓ c. cider vinegar
1 T. onion juice *or* ⅛ t. onion (grated)
1 t. salt
1 t. dry mustard
1½ T. poppy seeds

1. Combine all ingredients, except poppy seeds in blender.
2. Process on high speed until well blended.
3. Stir in poppy seeds.
4. Chill thoroughly. Stir well before serving.

Yield: 1¾ cups
Preparation: 5 minutes
Chill: 2-3 hours

"Serve over bed of assorted greens and sliced radishes or over fresh fruit! Enjoy!"

— NOTES —

STRAWBERRY MUFFINS
(Use Food Processor)

1½ c. flour
½ c. chilled butter (cut into 6 pieces)
¾ c. sugar
1 t. baking soda
¼ t. salt
2 eggs
¼ c. milk
2 t. sherry
½ c. walnuts
1 c. fresh strawberries (cut up)

1. In food processor bowl use knife blade. Add the flour, butter, sugar, soda, and salt.
2. Process for 10 seconds.
3. In small bowl, combine eggs and milk. Beat well. Add mixture to other ingredients. Process 10-15 seconds.
4. Add sherry. Turn processor on. Then off quickly.
5. Add nuts. Process 10 seconds. Add strawberries. Process 10 seconds.
6. Bake in small muffin cup pans at 350°F for 10-12 minutes or until just light brown. (If using regular muffin cup pans, bake 18-20 minutes.)

Makes: 36 small muffins or 18 regular
Preparation: 5 minutes
Cooking: 20 minutes

"The easiest muffins you'll ever make!"

— NOTES —

HERB BREAD

1 pkg. dry yeast
¼ c. lukewarm water
1 t. light brown sugar
1 T. butter (melted)
1 c. cottage cheese
1½ T. light brown sugar
1 t. salt
¼ t. baking soda
2 t. dill seed*
2½ c. unbleached flour (sifted)
melted butter
salt

1. In small bowl, sprinkle yeast over water. Stir in 1 t. light brown sugar. Let this mixture rest for 10 minutes until it puffs and bubbles a little.
2. Meanwhile, in large saucepan, combine butter, cottage cheese, 1 T. light brown sugar, salt, and baking soda. Heat mixture until lukewarm.
3. Remove from heat and stir in yeast mixture.
4. Fold in dill seed.
5. Place flour in food processor bowl. Pour slowly into bowl the contents of saucepan. Flour will absorb liquid. Mix until a stiff mass.
6. Let rise 1 hour in warm place. Cover lightly with moist towel.
7. Turn dough out on lightly floured board and knead for a few minutes.
8. Turn into 5x9″ loaf pan. Let rise 30-40 minutes or until it has risen above rim of pan.
9. Bake in oven preheated to 350°F for 40-45 minutes.
10. Brush top with butter and sprinkle with salt.

*To substitute for dill seed use fennel or caraway seeds, basil, tarragon, or oregano.

Makes: 5x9″ loaf
Preparation: 2 hours
Cooking: 45 minutes

"A most unusual taste — try with cream cheese lovingly spread on slices!"

— NOTES —

— NOTES —

The Little Inn Restaurant

— *Homosassa Springs* —

SPLIT-PEA SOUP
(Allow Peas to Soak Overnight)

1 c. split peas
2-4 c. water
1 carrot (diced)
1 small onion (diced)
ham bone
½ t. celery salt
½ t. garlic powder
salt and pepper to taste
3 c. milk

1. Wash peas several times then place them in pan with water and allow to soak overnight.
2. The next day add carrot, onion, and ham bone. Cook over medium heat until it boils. Simmer uncovered until peas are tender, about 1½ hours.
3. Remove ham bone and press the material through a seive. Return to pot with liquid they were cooked in. Add seasonings, milk, and any meat pieces from bone.
4. Heat through, stirring to thicken. Serve hot.

Serves: 4-6
Preparation: Soak overnight/10 minutes
Cooking: 2-3 hours

"Lip-smacking good with cornbread!"

— NOTES —

HONEY-LIME DRESSING

1 c. mayonnaise
½ c. honey
¾ t. paprika
1 t. celery seed
2-3 T. lime juice
1 drop green food coloring
1 20-oz. package frozen mixed fruit (or 1½ c. mixed fresh fruit)

1. Mix all ingredients together and refrigerate.
2. Pour over defrosted fruit. Serve.

Serves: 4
Preparation: 5 minutes
Chill: 2-3 hours

"A nice, cool and refreshing dessert!"

— NOTES —

CHICKEN PARMIGIAN

2	whole chicken breasts, split and de-boned
4	eggs (whipped)
½	c. bread crumbs
½	c. self-rising flour
1	T. garlic powder
½	t. paprika
1	t. white pepper
1	t. salt
4	slices Provolone cheese
2	c. spaghetti sauce (canned or homemade)

1. Blend bread crumbs, flour, and all seasonings together on a large dinner plate. Dip each chicken breast half into eggs, then into coating mix on plate.
2. Place chicken in a 5x7" baking dish. Bake at 350°F for 30 minutes or until done.
3. Place 1 chicken breast half on each dinner plate. Cover each with 1 slice Provolone cheese and ½ cup spaghetti sauce. Return plates to oven (or microwave) until cheese melts.

Serves: 4
Preparation: 15 minutes
Cooking: 30 minutes

"The coating mix for the chicken is great!... the extra can be refrigerated in a plastic bag for future use... Umm!"

— NOTES —

— NOTES —

The Blueberry Porch, Brooksville, Florida

R. STOCKEY

The Blueberry Patch

— *Brooksville* —

HOT CHICKEN SALAD SOUFFLE
(Allow to Refrigerate Overnight)

6   slices white bread
2½-3 lb. whole chicken (or 2 c. diced cooked chicken)
1   stalk celery (chopped)   — cook with whole chicken
1   small onion (chopped)
      salt to taste
½   c. celery (finely chopped)
½   c. onion (finely chopped)
½   c. green pepper (finely chopped)
½   c. salad dressing
½   c. cheddar cheese (shredded)
3   slightly beaten eggs
1½   c. milk
1   can cream of mushroom soup

1. Cook whole chicken with celery, onion, salt and
    enough water to halfway cover chicken. Cook until
    done, turning over halfway through cooking. Cool
    and dice 2 c. chicken.
2. Trim crusts from bread slices (save for future use)
    and place trimmed bread in bottom of 9 x 13″
    baking dish.
3. Combine the chicken, finely chopped celery, onion
    and green pepper with the salad dressing.
    Carefully spread oven bread slices.
4. Crumb or cube the reserved crusts and use as
    topping over chicken mixture. Sprinkle cheese over
    crusts.
5. Mix eggs and milk together. Pour over all
    ingredients in baking dish.
6. Refrigerate overnight.
7. Before baking, spoon can of soup over top and
    bake in 350 °F over for 1 hour.

Serves: 6-8
Preparation: 30 minutes — 1 hour
Cooking: 1 hour

*"Excellent for buffet entertaining! Don't plan on leftovers
— there won't be any!!"*

LEMON CLOUD PIE

8   oz. package cream cheese
1   c. powdered sugar
8   oz. container whipped topping (Cool Whip)
1   baked pie shell (or use butter-flavored 'ready-crust')
1   can lemon pie filling
   Cool Whip for topping

1. Soften cream cheese. Add powdered sugar and whip together.
2. Fold whipped topping into cream cheese mixture.
3. Layer cream cheese mixture in bottom of pie shell. Place lemon pie filling on top.
4. Refrigerate for 3-4 hours. Top each serving with Cool Whip, if desired.

Serves: 8
Preparation: 15 minutes
Chill: 3-4 hours

"Very, very easy! Elegant results...perfect for summer in Florida. No oven required."

— NOTES —

— NOTES —

The Four B's Restaurant

— *Ocala* —

HOT AND SPICY HOUSE DRESSING

2 c. catsup
1 T. sugar
1 t. fresh garlic (minced, in jar)
1 t. salt
1 t. black pepper
1 T. Worcestershire sauce
1 T. vinegar
½ t. paprika

1. Combine all ingredients in bowl and blend well.
2. Pour into quart jar and refrigerate until ready to use (refrigerate at least 4 hours).

Yield: 1½ pints
Preparation: 5 minutes
Chill: 4 hours (minimum)

"This lives up to its name!"

— NOTES —

FOUR B'S MUFFINS

1½ c. flour
2   t. baking powder
¼   t. salt
⅓   c. butter or margarine
½   c. milk
1   egg (beaten)
¼   c. sugar
1   c. carrots (finely grated)
½   t. pumpkin pie spice

1. Sift together flour, baking powder, salt into bowl.
   Cut in butter until it resembles coarse oatmeal.
2. Combine milk, egg, and sugar in smaller bowl.
   Pour into dry ingredients.
3. Add carrots and pumpkin pie spice. Mix until
   just moist (to overmix results in unrisen muffins).
4. Place in greased muffin pans.
5. Bake in 350°F oven for 20-30 minutes.

Makes: 1 dozen
Preparation: 15 minutes
Cooking: 30 minutes

"Very aromatic — good blend of flavors!"

— NOTES —

Palma Maria Restaurant

— Casselberry —

STUFFED FRESH ARTICHOKES

4	large globe artichokes
2-3	c. water
1	t. salt
1	T. lemon juice

— FILLING —

½	c. fresh white bread crumbs
2	T. fresh parsley (chopped)
1-2	cloves garlic (crushed)
	salt and pepper to taste
¾	c. Parmesan cheese
¾	c. fresh mushrooms (chopped) OR
	¾ c. crab meat OR
	2 hard boiled eggs (chopped)
	olive oil
	water for steaming

1. Cut off 1″ across top of artichokes and across bottom stem so they will sit flat in pan. Cut off tips of leaves to remove spines. Wash thoroughly.
2. In deep saucepan combine water, salt, and lemon juice. Bring to boil. Stand artichokes in pan. Cover and cook until barely tender (25-35 min.)
3. Drain. Discard some of the inner leaves and scoop out the hairy center "choke" with a teaspoon.

— FILLING —

4. Mix all ingredients together with just enough olive oil to moisten and hold ingredients together.
5. Spread artichoke leaves. Place ¼ of filling in each artichoke.
6. Place filled artichokes in shallow baking dish. Tie string around leaves to hold together. Add ½″ water to bottom of dish.
7. Sprinkle a little olive oil on top of each artichoke.

8. Cover pan tightly with aluminum foil. Bake in 350 °F. oven for 30-45 minutes, until tender.

Serves: 4
Preparation: 20 minutes
Cooking: 35/45 minutes

"You'll want to eat all 4 yourself ... a luscious treat."

— NOTES —

PALMA MARIA
ORLANDO

ORANGE SALAD

1   **orange**
1   **T. olive oil**
    fresh ground black pepper
    fresh mint leaves (chopped) or dried,
    crushed leaves

1.   Pare orange. Slice across in ⅛-¼" slices.
2.   Arrange slices on salad plate. Sprinkle olive oil over top, then pepper and mint leaves.
3.   Let stand 5 minutes. Serve immediately or refrigerate. (Best if refrigerated!)

Serves: 1
Preparation: 5 minutes
Chill: 30 minutes

"This looks delightful on a leaf of escarole or endive and tastes out of this world!"

— NOTES —

Mama Lo's

— *Gainesville* —

COLLARD GREENS

1   **bunch collard greens**
1   **T. shortening (Crisco)**
½   **T. butter**
½   **c. water**
1   **T. sugar**
1   **T. butter**
    salt and pepper to taste

1. Wash collard greens 3-4 times in running water until water runs clear. Then wash several more times to be sure they are clean (this is the secret to success as collards are **very** sandy!).
2. Chop collards very fine.
3. Heat shortening and butter until brown. Add collards and water.
4. Simmer for 1 hour. Watch so the pot doesn't go dry.
5. Add rest of ingredients. Serve.

Serves: 2-4
Preparation: 15 minutes
Cooking: 1½ hours

"Collards are a headless variety of cabbage that are rich in iron. Their appearance is similar to spinach but the flavor is unique. Their proper preparation is critical to maintain proper flavor!"

— NOTES —

STUFFED BELL PEPPERS

6	large, whole green peppers
1	lb. lean ground beef
½	onion (chopped)
½	c. ketchup
1	c. cooked rice (long grain white)
½	stalk celery (chopped)
	several dashes Worcestershire sauce
	salt and pepper to taste

— BROWN GRAVY —

2	c. water
4	T. butter
2	T. beef base (instant bouillon)
¼	t. garlic powder
4	T. cornstarch in ¼ c. water

1. Cut off ½-inch of peppers at stem end. Discard center stem. Chop remaining tops. Clean out peppers of seeds and pulp.
2. Combine chopped pepper with all remaining ingredients, mix well. Stuff into prepared peppers.
3. Place stuffed peppers in 9 x 11″ aluminum pan with 1 cup water in bottom. Cover with aluminum foil.
4. Bake in 350 °F. oven for 30 minutes. Cover with brown gravy and serve.

— BROWN GRAVY —
5. Place all ingredients, except corn starch and water mixture in sauce pan and bring to rapid boil.
6. Reduce heat and add cornstarch and water mixture. Heat until gravy reaches a thick consistency.

Serves: 6
Preparation: 15 minutes
Cooking: 30 minutes/15 minutes

"The brown gravy adds a nice touch to an old favorite."

BROCCOLI CASSEROLE

1   bunch broccoli, peeled and chopped
5   slices day old white bread, cut in cubes
5   eggs
¼   c. milk
4   T. butter
1   c. grated sharp cheddar cheese
1   t. salt
4   T. sugar

1. Lightly grease a 9 x 11" baking dish (or use pan with non-stick finish).
2. Place bread cubes in bottom of dish. Place broccoli on top of cubes.
3. Thoroughly mix together remaining ingredients. Pour over broccoli and bread.
4. Cover with aluminum foil. Bake for 35 minutes in 350°F oven.

Serves: 6
Preparation: 20 minutes
Cooking: 35 minutes

"A very different taste for broccoli."

— NOTES —

Malaga Street Depot

— *St. Augustine* —

GAZPACHO SOUP

2	28 oz. cans pear-shaped tomatoes
2	cucumbers (peeled, diced)
2	green peppers (diced)
1	medium onion (chopped, large chunks)
1	clove garlic
¼	c. olive oil
2	T. red wine vingar
2	t. fresh thyme
2	t. fresh oregano
2	t. fresh Cilantro (Chinese parsley — may substitute fresh parsley if not available)
2	t. fresh parsley
2	t. ground cumin
	salt and pepper to taste
	Jalapeno peppers (optional)
	garlic croutons
	scallions (sliced)

1. Crush tomatoes with hand in large bowl.
2. Add all other ingredients except croutons and scallions.
3. Chill. Dish into bowls and garnish with croutons and scallions.

Serves: 4
Preparation: 20 minutes
Chill: 2-3 hours

"If at all possible, use fresh herbs as it is more flavorful!"

— NOTES —

PESTO SAUCE

½ c. fresh parsley (chopped fine)
½ c. fresh basil (chopped fine)
½ c. Parmesan cheese (grated fresh)
1   T. lemon juice
2   t. fresh garlic (minced)
½ - ¾ c. olive oil
    salt and pepper to taste

1. Mix parsley, basil, Parmesan cheese, lemon juice, and garlic together.
2. Add olive oil until mixture is the thickness of ketchup.
3. Add salt and pepper. Keep on hand for seasoning. The longer sauce sits the better it tastes.

*NOTE: Will last in refrigerator for several months, so make up a batch!

"Adds a great taste to vegetables. We especially like it combined with fresh broccoli."

— NOTES —

BREAKFAST TACOS

2	eggs (beaten)
¼	c. green peppers (diced)
¼	c. onions (diced)
1	corn tortilla
3	T. refried beans
⅓	c. cheddar cheese (shredded)
	picante sauce

— PICANTE SAUCE —

1	green pepper (diced)
1	small onion (diced)
3-4	Jalapeno peppers (minced)
1	clove garlic (crushed)
28	oz. can pear-shaped tomatoes (crushed with hand)
1	T. + 1 t. cider vinegar
2	t. oregano
1	bay leaf
	dash ground cumin
1	T. + 1 t. fresh Cilantro (may substitute fresh parsley)
	juice of one lemon

— PICANTE SAUCE —

1. Mix all ingredients for sauce together.

— TACOS —

2. Combine eggs, green pepper, and onions on griddle or in saute pan. Cook.
3. Heat corn tortilla briefly on griddle.
4. Place tortilla on plate. Top with eggs and refried beans. Fold in sides to seal.
5. Top with cheese and liberal amount of picante sauce.
6. Place under broiler for few seconds.

NOTE: The picante sauce can be kept in the refrigerator for future use. You will find many uses for it (great for dipping tortilla chips).

Serves: 1
Preparation: 15 minutes for sauce/5 minutes for tacos
Cooking: 5 minutes

"A most unusual breakfast dish!"

— NOTES —

BROCCOLI TOSKA
("Inside Out Omelet")

8-10 4"spears fresh broccoli (can use ¾ pkg. frozen)
½   c. water
4   eggs
2-2½ T. pesto sauce (See recipe on page 191)
2   t. Parmesan cheese
½   c. flour
2   T. olive oil
2   T. butter
      fresh garlic (crushed)
½   lemon
⅓   c. sherry
1½   T. flour
⅓   c. broccoli broth (saved from cooking broccoli)
3   oz. (1 c.) Swiss cheese (shredded)
Optional: 1 c. hollandaise sauce (pkg. mix makes 1 c. —
      follow directions)

1. Cook broccoli al dente in shallow pan in ½ cup water. Remove broccoli and save broth.
2. In small bowl mix eggs, pesto sauce, and Parmesan cheese.
3. Lightly flour broccoli spears. Drop into egg batter bowl.
4. In a 9" or 10" skillet or saute pan (best with non-stick surface) heat olive oil and butter.
5. Pour broccoli and egg batter into skillet. Cook until quite brown on outside edge.
6. Carefully turn over and sprinkle touch of garlic on top. Next, add juice of lemon and sherry. Sprinkle flour into liquids around edges of pan.
7. Add broccoli broth. Shake pan to get liquid to thicken a little around edges of egg.
8. Place Swiss cheese over top. Slide under broiler briefly to melt cheese and brown.
9. Cut and place on plates. Salt and pepper. Top with hollandaise sauce, if desired.

Serves: 2-6 (depending on if it is to be entree or
    side dish)
Preparation: 30 minutes
Cooking: 30 minutes

"Bon Appetit! Most unusual but yummy!"

— NOTES —

— NOTES —

Cafe
Anastasia

— *St. Augustine* —

OYSTERS GIOVANNI

2	c. crushed Ritz crackers (approx. 45 crackers)
¾	c. scallions (chopped)
2	t. garlic (minced)
½	c. fresh parsley (chopped)
2	t. dillweed
1	pt. oysters (drained well)
30	oyster shells or 6 ramekins
3	lemons
	cognac
½	c. clarified butter

1. Mix crackers, scallions, garlic, parsley and dillweed together.
2. Place well drained oysters in shells or ramekins.
3. Squeeze lemons over oysters and add a few drops of cognac to each shell.
4. Cover generously with cracker mixture and pour butter on top of all.
5. Place under broiler (rack should be in second position from the top).
6. Cook until golden brown, about 3-5 minutes.

Serves: 5-6 as appetizer
Preparation: 10 minutes
Cooking: 5 minutes

"An oyster lover's delight!"

— NOTES —

SHRIMP MOUTARDE

2	T. butter
2	T. scallions (chopped)
1	t. garlic (chopped)
1	T. lemon juice
1	T. Dijon mustard
½	c. dry white wine (use good brand)
½	c. whipping cream
1	lb. medium-large shrimp (shelled and cleaned)

1. In large pan over high heat, saute scallions and garlic in butter.
2. Add lemon juice, mustard, and white wine. Reduce 15 seconds.
3. Add cream. Bring to boil.
4. Add shrimp (don't crowd!). Cook for 2-3 minutes. Remove with slotted spoon. Cook remaining shrimp.
5. Continue stirring sauce until it thickens. Pour sauce over shrimp.

Serves: 4
Preparation: 15 minutes
Cooking: 10 minutes

"An easy but elegant dish. Serve over rice and with a pretty green vegetable!"

— NOTES —

FISH BANANA CURRY

4	fillets, medium thickness (Red Snapper preferred)
1	egg (beaten)
½	c. milk
2	bananas (cut in half and sliced down middle)
	curry powder
¼	c. flour
1	T. Crisco oil
1	T. olive oil
4	T. butter
1	lemon
	sherry
¼	c. fresh parsley (chopped)

1. Place fillets in mixture of egg and milk. Remove. Place on dinner plate. Prepare bananas and place along sides.
2. Generously sprinkle curry powder over fish and bananas. Lightly flour.
3. In large saute pan, over high heat, heat oils and 1 T. butter. Place bananas, flat side down in pan. Saute until golden brown.
4. Turn bananas over. Sprinkle lemon juice and sherry on each. Transfer to dinner plates.
5. Add fillets to pan, skin side up. Cook for few minutes. Turn over and sprinkle lemon and sherry on each. Transfer to plates.
6. In small pan heat 3 T. butter, parsley, and lemon juice. Pour over fillets on dinner plates.

Serves: 4
Preparation: 10 minutes
Cooking: 5 minutes

"The curry taste is delicious with Snapper. Chutney is a nice complement."

CHOCOLATE MOUSSE

5	1-oz. squares unsweetened chocolate
1	T. butter
¼	t. vanilla extract
1	large orange
1	c. sugar
6	eggs
	whipped cream
	Cointreau

1. Break up chocolate. Melt slowly in double boiler with butter and vanilla.
2. Meanwhile, squeeze orange and add juice to sugar in a small saucepan. Heat until sugar is dissolved, stirring occasionally.
3. Separate eggs, placing whites in refrigerator.
4. In large mixing bowl, beat egg yolks while slowly adding in the syrup. Continue beating until thick and lightly colored (10-20 minutes).
5. Fold melted chocolate into egg yolk mixture.
6. Beat egg whites until stiff peaks form. Gently and carefully fold one-quarter of the egg whites into the chocolate mixture. Fold in the remaining three-quarters.
7. Carefully place mousse into individual dessert dishes. Chill 3-5 hours. Top with whipped cream and Cointreau.

Serves: 8
Preparation: 30 minutes
Cooking: 15 minutes
Chill: 3-5 hours

"A rich dessert with a lovely hint of orange!"

The Vilano Seafood Shack, Vilano Beach, Florida

P. Stockey

The Vilano
Seafood
Shack

— *Vilano Beach* —

THE SHACK'S STUFFED MUSHROOMS

1	lb. fresh mushrooms (largest you can find)
2	slices whole wheat bread
4	T. butter
¼	c. celery (minced)
¼	c. onions (minced)
¼	t. oregano
⅛	t. thyme
1¼	t. Worcestershire sauce
⅛	t. salt
¼	t. pepper
2	dashes tabasco sauce
1	c. crab meat (frozen or canned)
	paprika
	lemon wedges (garnish)
⅛	of a Datil pepper (minced)
	(may substitute very hot peppers)

1. Remove stems from mushrooms. Place caps in shallow baking dish.
2. Remove crusts from bread. Crumble remaining bread in bowl. In small skillet place 2 T. butter and saute celery and onions until tender. Add to bowl with bread.
4. Add all spices, 2 T. melted butter, and crab meat. Mix well.
5. Stuff mushrooms, mounding well using all stuffing. Sprinkle with paprika.
6. Bake in 350°F oven for 12-15 minutes. Garnish with lemon wedges.

Makes: 8-12
Preparation: 15 minutes
Cooking: 15 minutes

"Great for an appetizer or accompaniment to a fine meal."

NATHAN'S SAUTEED SNAPPER VILANO

½   c. butter
4   snapper fillets (or any white fish fillets)
      flour for dusting
½   lemon
1   t. sherry (use a good brand)
1   T. capers

1. Heat butter in skillet until it just begins to boil.
3. Cook each side 3-5 minutes, depending on thickness.
4. When cooked on both sides, squeeze lemon over fillets and add sherry and capers.
5. Allow edges of fish to crispen. Serve by spooning capers over fillets.

Serves: 4
Preparation: 5 minutes
Cooking: 5 minutes

"The sherry and capers add the zing — easy!"

— NOTES —

CINDY'S FISH SPREAD

1   lb. fish (flaked) from large fish carcasses OR
     1 lb. fresh fillets (2 c. — flaked and cooked)
1   c. sour cream
¼   c. onion (chopped)
2-3 dashes tabasco
1-2 dashes Worcestershire sauce
     lots of salt and pepper to taste
2-3 drops Liquid Smoke
     crackers

1. Flake fish fillets, or, if using fish from carcasses steam in basket over boiling water for 15 minutes until fish loosens from bones (the tastiest meat is out of the jawbones). Pick out meat.
2. Add sour cream to meat until spreading consistency.
3. Add remaining ingredients. Mix well.
4. Spread on wafer crackers. Escort brand is an excellent choice.
5. You may substitute crab meat for fish.

Serves: 12-15 as an appetizer
Preparation: 15 minutes

"The consistency is heavenly. . . an easy party dish."

— NOTES —

P. Stickey

Whitey's Fish Camp, Orange Park, Florida

Whitey's
Fish Camp

— *Orange Park* —

CATFISH CHOWDER

1½ lbs. fresh water catfish
2   quarts of water
¼   lb. salt pork (or bacon)
2   medium onions (chopped)
2   medium potatoes (diced)
1   T. Accent
     tabasco to taste
     salt and pepper to taste

1. Clean and wash catfish. Cook in 2 quarts water until fish starts to come away from bone (about 15-20 minutes).
2. Meanwhile fry salt pork until crisp. Chop and set aside with drippings.
3. Carefully remove fish from bones. Return boned fish, and all other ingredients to pot.
4. Bring back to boil and simmer until potatoes and onions are tender, about 10-15 minutes.

Makes: 2 quarts
Preparation: 15 minutes
Cooking: 30-40 minutes

"Make up a batch to put in the freezer! You'll love it!"

— NOTES —

SWEET 'N SOUR COLE SLAW

1   small head green cabbage (shredded)
2   medium carrots (grated)
1   c. sugar
1   c. vinegar
½   c. water
½   c. salad oil
1   T. celery seed
1   T. Accent
    salt and pepper to taste
    Optional: Purple cabbage and/or green pepper

1.   Mix all above ingredients well.
2.   Let stand for 1 hour before serving.

Serves: 4-5
Preparation: 20 minutes
Chill: 1 hour

"The name describes it all!"

— NOTES —

— NOTES —

Beignets

— *Jacksonville* —

RED BEANS
(Allow To Soak Overnight)

1	lb. dry kidney beans (red beans)
2	large onions (chopped)
2	cloves garlic (minced)
1	bay leaf
¼	t. cumin powder
1	t. parsley
	dash or two of hot pepper sauce
1	T. sugar
	salt and pepper to taste
	dash Worcestershire sauce
1	lb. sausage and/or diced ham

1. Soak beans overnight in 4 c. water in large saucepan. Rinse several times. Cover well with water.
2. Add onions, garlic, and bay leaf. Simmer for at least 2 hours or until beans are tender and soft.
3. Add remaining ingredients and cook for ½ hour more. Serve over rice or with buttery tasting crackers along side.

Serves: 4
Preparation: overnight soaking/10 minutes
Cooking: 3 hours

"On cold chilly nights, a great body warmer!"

— NOTES —

SHRIMP CREOLE

2	lbs. medium shrimp (in shells)
2¼	c. water
2	T. butter
2	T. flour
½	large onion (diced)
1	green pepper (diced)
2	cloves garlic (minced)
½	c. tomato paste
2	T. fresh parsley (minced)
3-4	scallions (cut crosswise)
	salt and pepper to taste

1. Shell and clean shrimp. Place shells in water and cook to make stock. Put shrimp aside.
2. In large skillet, brown butter, add flour and stir to make paste.
3. Brown onions, green pepper, and garlic in skillet with paste.
4. Drain stock from shells and add 2 c. of stock to skillet along with tomato paste. Cook for 1 hour or until thick.
5. Add shrimp, parsley, scallions, salt and pepper.
6. Cook until shrimp are tender. Do not overcook. Serve over rice.

Serves: 6
Preparation: 15 minutes
Cooking: 1½ hours

"A colorful dish with a taste to match!"

— NOTES —

CHICKEN JAMBALAYA

3	T. butter
3	T. flour
2	large onions (chopped)
1	bunch scallions (chopped)
1	red pepper (chopped)
2	T. parsley (fresh best)
¼	t. basil
	salt and pepper
	several dashes hot sauce
3	c. water
3	chicken bouillon cubes
2	lbs. cooked white chicken (cubed-about 3-4 c.)

1. Brown butter in large skillet. Stir in flour and blend to make paste.
2. Add vegetables and brown. Add spices, seasonings, water, and bouillon cubes. Simmer for 1 hour.
3. Add chicken and thicken with equal amounts of butter and flour if necessary. Heat through.
4. Serve over white rice, dirty rice, or mixed white and wild rice.

Serves: 4
Preparation: 10 minutes
Cooking: 1 hour 10 minutes

"The red pepper adds a delightful color to a most enchanting dish!"

— NOTES —

— NOTES —

Hopkins Boarding House, Pensacola, Florida

Hopkins
Boarding
House

— *Pensacola* —

FRIED SQUASH

**2   lbs. yellow squash (may substitute zucchini)
salt
self-rising flour
fat for deep fat frying**

1. Wash and slice squash into 1″ pieces.
2. Sprinkle salt over squash so that all pieces are
   lightly salted. (The salt draws out the extra liquid.)
3. Let sit 1 hour. Pour off liquid.
4. Dip and completely cover each piece in
   self-rising flour.
5. Fry in deep fat at 350 °F until brown and crisp.

Serves: 6
Preparation: 1 hour 15 minutes
Cooking: 10 minutes

"A nice change for an old favorite!"

— NOTES —

SWEET POTATO SOUFFLE

**4   c. mashed sweet potatoes (if potatoes are dry,
      add up to ½ c. evaporated milk)**
½   c. sugar
½   c. butter or oleo
½   c. coconut
⅓   c. raisins
1   t. lemon extract or orange peel
miniature marshmallows

1.   While potatoes are hot, add all other ingredients.
2.   Place in casserole dish. Cover with marshmallows.
3.   Bake in 300°F oven until marshmallows are brown,
     20-30 minutes.

Serves: 6
Preparation: 10 minutes
Cooking: 30 minutes

*"A nice accompaniment with smoked ham and perky
green vegetables!"*

— NOTES —

CHICKEN NOODLE CASSEROLE

1	stewing chicken
8	oz. pkg. flat egg noodles
16	oz. can tomato sauce
8	oz. can tomato paste
2	onions (chopped)
1	green pepper (chopped)
½	c. celery (chopped)
2	t. oregano
	salt and pepper to taste

1. Place stewing chicken in large pot. Cover with water and simmer until tender.
2. Remove chicken from broth and let cool. Set aside.
3. Cook noodles in broth until almost tender. Add remaining ingredients, cover, and simmer until vegetables are tender.
4. While vegetables are cooking, remove bones from chicken and return chicken to pot just before vegetables are done.

Serves: 6
Preparation: 30 minutes
Cooking: 1½ hours

"An inexpensive meal that rates a 10!"

— NOTES —

SQUASH CASSEROLE

3   lbs. summer squash (use small size)
¼   c. water
1   t. salt
½   c. onion (chopped)
½   c. butter
2   eggs (beaten)
¾   c. crushed Saltines
    salt and pepper to taste

1. Wash and trim squash. Cook in saucepan with water and salt until tender. Drain and mash.
2. Saute onion in butter until tender. Add to squash. Add eggs, Saltines, salt, and pepper. Mix and put in buttered casserole dish.
3. Bake in 325 °F oven for 20 minutes.

Serves: 6
Preparation: 10 minutes
Cooking: 30 minutes

"The small, young squash have the best flavor!"

— NOTES —

BROCCOLI CASSEROLE

10 oz. pkg. frozen broccoli (chopped)
1 stalk celery (diced)
1 onion (diced)
½ c. butter or margarine
1 c. cooked rice
1 c. cheddar cheese (shredded)
1 c. cream of mushroom soup
salt and pepper to taste

1. Cook broccoli in small amount of water until done. Drain.
2. Saute celery, and onion in butter.
3. Mix remaining ingredients in casserole dish. Bake in 350 °F oven until bubbly, about 30 minutes.

Serves: 6
Preparation: 5 minutes
Cooking: 35 minutes

"An easy vegetable casserole that can be prepared the night before and baked just before serving!"

— NOTES —

Canary
Cottage
Restaurant

— Panama City —

WILTED SPINACH DELIGHT

½ lb. bacon
½-¾ c. sugar (or sugar substitute)
2 T. dry mustard
1 c. vinegar
¼ c. water
1 lb. fresh spinach (washed, cleaned, torn into bite-size pieces)
3 tomatoes (cut in wedges)
½ c. scallions (sliced)
2 hard boiled eggs (chopped fine)
½ c. sharp cheddar cheese
12 fresh mushrooms (sliced)

1. Place bacon in frying pan and fry until crisp. Remove bacon and allow to cool. Crumble. Set aside.
2. Add sugar, dry mustard, and vinegar to bacon drippings. Stir to blend. Add water. Stir. Bring to boil. Simmer 5 minutes while arranging salads.
3. Place spinach on salad plates. Arrange the other ingredients on top including the crumbled bacon.
4. Spoon the hot sauce over and serve immediately.

Variation: Use yellow squash which has been sliced thin.

Serves: 4-6
Preparation: 20 minutes
Cooking: 10 minutes

"A technicolor delight!"

— NOTES —

RAVIOLI VERDI

1	lb. frozen ravioli
½	c. butter (melted)
10	oz. pkg. fresh spinach (washed, stems removed)
4	oz. Romano cheese (grated)
½	lb. Ricotta cheese
	— SAUCE —
2	T. butter
2	T. cornstarch
2	c. milk
¼	t. lemon extract
	salt and pepper to taste

— SAUCE —

1. In saucepan place butter and melt. Blend in cornstarch to a paste. Slowly add milk while stirring. Cook over low heat until thickened.
2. Add lemon extract, salt and pepper. Stir.

— ASSEMBLY —

3. Allow ravioli to defrost on their own.
4. Pour melted butter into bottom of 9x13″ cake pan.
5. Place layer of ravioli (⅓) across bottom of pan. Follow with layer (⅓) of spinach. Sprinkle ⅓ of Romano cheese across spinach. Dot with ½ of Ricotta cheese. Add ½ of sauce.
6. Repeat layers another time.
7. Finish off with last of ravioli and spinach.
8. Sprinkle Romano cheese over all. Cover with aluminum foil.
9. Bake in 350°F oven for 1 hour.

   Variations: If you have leftover spaghetti sauce use instead of cream sauce. You can also use thin slices of ham.

Serves: 6-8
Preparation: 30 minutes
Cooking: 20 minutes/1 hour

"A most unusual but tasty lasagna-type dish!"

SPANISH CHOPPED BEEF CASSEROLE

2   lbs. ground round (can substitute ground chuck)
1   lb. ground sausage
1   green pepper (diced)
1   medium onion (diced)
2   carrots (diced)
3   stalks celery (diced)
16 oz. can tomato sauce
10 dashes tabasco sauce
    dash of granulated garlic
    salt and pepper to taste
15 oz. can red kidney beans, drained
15 oz. can whole kernel corn
½   c. water
½   c. shredded cheddar cheese
2   pkgs. corn muffin mix

1. In large fry pan brown meats. Add green pepper,
    onion, carrots, and celery. Cook until tender.
2. Add other ingredients except corn muffin mix. Stir
    and mix well.
3. Pour into large casserole.
4. Make corn muffin mix according to package
    directions. Pour over top of casserole.
5. Bake in 350°F oven for 30 minutes or until golden
    brown.

Serves: 8
Preparation: 20 minutes
Cooking: 45 minutes

"A whole delicious and colorful meal in a casserole!"

— NOTES —

KING'S CHOCOLATE

1 **Duncan Hines Devil's Food Cake Mix**
2 **eggs**
1½ **c. water (minus 2 t.)**
2 **t. lemon extract**
14 **oz. dry chocolate frosting mix**
2 **c. boiling water**
  whipped cream topping

1. Mix cake mix, eggs, water, and lemon extract in large bowl according to package directions.
2. Grease 9x13x2½" baking dish. Pour in cake mix.
3. Sprinkle dry frosting mix over batter. **Very carefully,** pour the boiling water over the ingredients in the dish.
4. Bake in 350°F oven for 30-40 minutes. Allow to cool until warm. Cut into squares. Place gently onto dessert plates. Top with whipped cream.

Makes: 9x11" cake
Preparation: 5 minutes
Cooking: 40 minutes

Variations: Use your imagination!
    Chocolate cake — rum extract — lemon frosting
    Cherry cake — rum extract — chocolate frosting
    Vanilla cake — brandy — vanilla frosting
    Orange cake — lemon extract — chocolate frosting

"An ancient Greek dish. It certainly must have been invented on Mt. Olympus!"

— NOTES —

— NOTES —

Spring Creek Restaurant

— Spring Creek —

CHEESE STUFFED TOMATOES

3   large tomatoes (hearty type)
3   sausage patties (cooked, crumbled) or 5 slices
    bacon cooked and crumbled
    drippings from sausage or bacon
4   oz. Jalapeno cheese (grated)
½   c. green pepper (diced)
½   c. onion (diced)
¼   c. dry onion flakes
½   t. granulated garlic
½   t. seasoned salt
2   T. sugar
2   c. croutons (may substitute day-old bread cubes or
    cracker pieces)
    chili powder

1. Wash tomatoes. Cut in half and scoop out pulp.
    Place halves in baking dish.
2. Place pulp in large bowl. Add all of the above
    ingredients except chili powder. Mix well.
3. Stuff tomato halves, mounding the stuffing.
    Sprinkle with chili powder.
4. Bake in 350°F oven for 15 minutes.

Serves: 6
Preparation: 20 minutes
Cooking: 15 minutes

"It's easy to make a meal of these!"

— NOTES —

FRIED CORN

6   ears fresh corn (at room temperature)
3   lbs. "all-purpose" cooking fat
(or enough to cover corn)

1. Pull husks and silk from corn. Break ears in half.
2. Heat fat for deep fat frying to 350 °F in a 3-4 quart kettle. Test for temperature with thermometer. If you don't have one, drop a 1-inch bread cube into hot fat. If cube browns in 60 seconds the fat will be about 350 °F.
3. Very carefully drop corn into fat. Cook until ears are brown and crunchy on outside kernels.

Serves: 4-6
Preparation: 5 minutes
Cooking: 10 minutes

"A fun way to serve corn!"

— NOTES —

175

SPRING CREEK JALAPENO CHEESE GRITS

4 c. water
1 t. salt
1 c. grits
¼ c. margarine
4 oz. Jalapeno cheese (diced)
1 egg (beaten)
⅓ c. evaporated milk
2 dashes tabasco sauce
¼ c. bread crumbs
paprika

1. In large saucepan, heat water and salt to boiling.
   Add grits.
2. Reduce heat and slowly cook until almost done.
   Stir several times.
3. Add margarine and cheese. Stir until melted.
4. Add egg, milk, and tabasco sauce. Stir until
   well mixed.
5. Grease a 1½-quart casserole. Add grits. Cover top
   with bread crumbs. Sprinkle with paprika.
6. Bake at 350°F for 30 minutes.

Serves: 6
Preparation: 10 minutes
Cooking: 20-30 minutes

"Spicy and hot...you'll love it!"

— NOTES —

FRIED MULLET AND BACKBONE

4   **mullet fillets (from small to medium fish)**
     seasoned salt
1   **c. cracker meal**
     oil for frying
     backbone with tail attached from fillets

1. Sprinkle mullet fillets with seasoned salt.
2. Pat cracker meal on fillets to cover.
3. Heat oil to 350°F. Deep fat fry fillets for 10 minutes.
4. Take fishback and tail bones and dip in cracker meal. Fry for 5 minutes.
5. Serve fillets and backbones together.

Serves: 2-4
Preparation: 10 minutes
Cooking: 20 minutes

"This dish is unique to the area. They eat the meat off the bones along with the cracker meal. Try it before passing judgment!"

— NOTES —

CHOCOLATE PEANUT BUTTER PIE

1½ c. sugar
¼ c. cornstarch
1 t. flour
⅔ c. cocoa (or 3 squares unsweetened melted chocolate)
¼ t. salt
2¼ c. whole milk
¾ c. evaporated milk
4 egg yolks, beaten well
1 t. butter
1¼ t. vanilla
1 9″ baked pie shell, cooled
1-1½ c. chunky style peanut butter
whipped cream (topping)

1. In medium saucepan, mix sugar, cornstarch, flour, cocoa, salt. Stir until well mixed.
2. Blend the milks together. Pour a little at a time into the saucepan until consistency of a smooth paste. Add remaining milk, stirring well.
3. Add egg yolks and butter. Cook over low heat, stirring constantly until thickened.
4. Remove from heat, add vanilla, stir well. Set aside to cool.
5. Spread peanut butter over the bottom of cooled pie shell and up sides of shell.
6. Pour cooled chocolate mixture into pie shell and refrigerate.
7. Cut into serving portions and top with whipped cream.

Serves: 8
Preparation: 15 minutes/1 hour to chill
Cooking: 20 minutes
Chill: 2 hours

"A creamy, delicious and unusual dessert!"

— NOTES —

Wakulla Springs Lodge, Wakulla Springs, Florida

Wakulla
Springs
Lodge

— *Wakulla Springs* —

NAVY BEAN SOUP

1	lb. dried navy beans
5	c. water
1	can beef consomme
1	chicken bouillon cube
4	potatoes (diced)
2	onions (diced)
¼	c. butter
4	carrots
2	c. chopped ham
3	bay leaves
	salt and pepper to taste

1. Place navy beans, water, consomme, and bouillon cube in large pot. Bring to boil and then simmer for 2 hours.
2. Add potatoes to soup pot. Saute onions in butter until partially cooked. Add to soup pot along with everything else.
3. Simmer 1 hour or until vegetables are done. Serve.

Serves: 6
Preparation: 15 minutes
Cooking: 3 hours

"Serve with Cuban bread and green salad for a very nutritious meal!"

— NOTES —

CRAB IMPERIAL

1   lb. crab meat (best to use fresh — pick through to remove cartilage)
2   stalks celery (minced)
⅓   c. mayonnaise
1   t. lemon juice (fresh)
¼   t. salt
¼   t. Accent
2   dashes Worcestershire sauce
½   t. granulated garlic
     cracker crumbs
     Parmesan cheese

1. Butter casserole dish. Combine all ingredients above, except bread crumbs and cheese, in bowl. Mix well.
2. Let sit 1 hour. Place in buttered casserole dish. Top with cracker crumbs, Parmesan cheese. Dot with butter.
3. Bake in 350°F oven for 20 minutes.

Serves: 4
Preparation: 1 hour 15 minutes
Cooking: 20 minutes

"A light and delicate casserole!"

— NOTES —

STUFFED CORNISH HENS SUPREME
WITH WILD RICE

2 Cornish hens
½ bunch scallions (chopped)
½ c. fresh mushrooms (chopped)
1 c. prepared bread crumbs
⅓ c. sour cream
1 hard boiled egg (chopped)
salt and pepper
garlic butter

— SUPREME SAUCE —
drippings from hens
½ c. butter
¼ c. scallions (chopped)
½ c. fresh mushrooms (sliced)
½ c. flour
milk
salt and pepper
½ t. granulated garlic
½ t. nutmeg

— WILD RICE —
1 pkg. wild rice
water
butter

— BIRDS —
1. Clean and rinse birds. Mix scallions, mushrooms, bread crumbs, sour cream, and egg together in bowl.
2. Gently stuff birds making sure not to pack stuffing too tightly.
3. Salt and pepper birds. Apply garlic butter to outside of birds. Place breast side up in flat baking dish.
4. Cover dish with aluminum foil and bake in 350 °F oven for 45 minutes.

5. At the end of cooking time, remove the foil drain drippings and put birds back to brown.

— SUPREME SAUCE —

6. Combine drippings and butter in small saute pan. Saute scallions and mushrooms until tender.
7. Add flour, stir until paste is formed. Add milk until desired sauce consistency.
8. Add seasonings.

— WILD RICE —

9. Cook rice according to package directions using proper amounts of water and butter.
10. Serve cornish hens on bed of wild rice with supreme sauce over top.

Serves: 2-4
Preparation: 20 minutes
Cooking: 1 hour

"A delightful dish that any cook would be proud to serve!"

— NOTES —

KEY LIME CHESS PIE

2	cups sugar
1	tablespoon flour
1	tablespoon corn meal
	Dash of salt
4	eggs
½	stick (¼ cup) butter or margarine, melted
¼	cup milk
¼	cup Key lime or Persian lime juice, strained
1	9-inch pastry shell, unbaked (see page 18)

Preheat the oven to 375°. Combine the sugar, flour, corn meal, and salt, tossing lightly. Add the eggs, butter, milk, and lime juice. Beat with an electric mixer at medium speed for 5 minutes. Pour into the pastry shell. Bake for 35-45 minutes or until the filling is set and top is golden brown. Cut while warm.

Yield: 1 9-inch pie

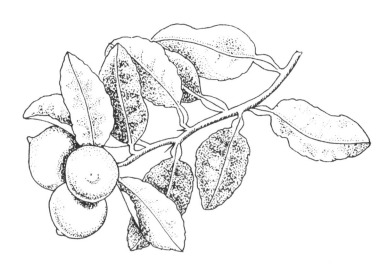

GLOSSARY OF TERMS

Al dente — To cook until barely tender, such as pasta.

Blanch — To parboil and then shock in cold water.

Bechamel (see Cream Sauce)

Brown Sauce/Sauce Espanole — A rich beef stock reduced and thickened with roux. May be purchased as beef gravy.

Beurre Manie — 1 t. flour mixed with 1 t. butter — for thickening soups and sauces. Make a dozen of these little balls and freeze to be used as needed.

Butterfly — To cut against the grain or cut lengthwise, leaving meat attached on one side. This is done for appearance and to tenderize.

Caramelize — To melt sugar until it is liquid and light brown.

Chop/Dice/Mince —
Chop = ¼" cubes
Dice = ⅛" cubes
Mince = smallest cubes

Clarify/Clarified — To make butter clear by heating and removing all whey or sediment as it rises to the top. Then carefully strain.

Court Bouillon — Highly seasoned fish broth (see fish stock).

Cream Sauce/or Bechamel — White sauce made with milk.
1 T. butter
1 cup hot milk
1 T. flour
salt, pepper, nutmeg to taste
1. Make roux of butter and flour. Cook until frothy, about 2 minutes.
2. Remove from heat. Slowly whisk in hot milk until smooth.
3. Cook 1 minute more and season.

Yield: 1 cup

Cream Sauce is Bechamel made with cream instead of milk.

Veloute is Bechamel made with white stock (such as chicken, veal or fish) in place of milk.

Crepes — Thin pancakes (use blender or food processor)
3-4 eggs
1 cup flour
1½ cups milk
½ t. salt
3 T. butter (melted)
1. Combine all ingredients in processor and blend until smooth. Allow batter to rest 1 hour before frying. May be kept in refrigerator for 1 week.
2. 2 T. for each crepe in a 6-inch pan.

De-glaze — To pour liquid (such as wine, water or stock) in a cooking pan, scraping sides and bottom to loosen residue used in sauce.

Demi-Glaze — Half-glaze/A reduced brown sauce.

Dredge/Dust/Flour — To dip in or sprinkle lightly with flour.

Fillet/Filet — Boneless meat or fish. To remove bones from fish.

Fish Stock/Court Bouillon — Trimmings and scraps from fish
1-2 onions
parsley stems, 1 carrot, 1 stalk celery
1 cup white wine
2 cups water
1. Simmer 20 minutes and strain.

Flambe/Flame — To cover food lightly with spirits and carefully ignite. It is to add flavor or spectacular beauty when serving.

Hollandaise Sauce (Blender)
3 egg yolks
dash of cayenne
2 t. lemon juice
½ cup butter (melted)
¼ t. salt
1. In blender or food processor, beat yolks until thickened. Beat in juice, salt and cayenne.
2. Pour in hot butter, in a stream with machine running. Serve in a warmed bowl.
Yield: 1 cup

Hollandaise Sauce (Classic)
¾ cup butter
4 t. lemon juice
3 egg yolks (beaten)
dash of salt & cayenne
1. In top of double boiler, melt ⅓ butter. Beat in eggs and juice with wire whisk.
2. Add remaining butter slowly, beating constantly until mixture thickens — never allowing water to boil.
3. Stir in seasonings and serve.

Yield: ¾ cup

Julienne — To cut into thin matchstick-like strips.

Poach — To simmer gently in hot liquid, to cover.

Puree — To force food through a sieve or blend in food processor until smooth.

Reduce — To cook or simmer a liquid until it is less; to concentrate flavor.

Roux — An equal amount of butter and flour cooked a few minutes until smooth. Used to thicken.

Saute — To cook in shallow pan, in small amount of butter or fat.

Score — To make shallow cuts in surface of meat.

Zest — Grated rind of citrus.

Index

FAMOUS FLORIDA! ®

FAMOUS FLORIDA!® SERIES

    SeaSide Publishing offers a luscious harvest in the slim volumes that make up our *Famous Florida!* cookbook series. Each offers a generous serving of the state's unique bounty and heritage: crab, conch, seafood, Key lime, orange and Seminole Indian recipes.

    This series is a repository of specialties from some of the best restaurants in the state. Many of the creations are found nowhere else.